TEACHING INFORMATION TECHNOLOGY SKILLS: The Big6™ in Elementary Schools

By Michael B. Eisenberg and Robert E. Berkowitz

With Barbara A. Jansen and Tami J. Little

A Publication of THE BOOK REPORT & LIBRARY TALK
Professional Growth Series

Linworth Publishing, Inc.
Worthington, Ohio

Library of Congress Cataloging-in-Publication Data

Eisenberg, Michael B.
    Teaching information & technology skills: The Big6 in elementary schools/ by Michael B. Eisenberg and Robert E.
Berkowitz: with Barbara A. Jansen and Tami J. Little.
                p.   cm.
    Includes biographical references (p. ix) and index.
    ISBN 0-938865-81-1
    1. Informational retrevial—Study and teaching (Elementary)
    2. Instructional retrival—Study and teaching (Elementary)—United States
    3. Electronic information resource literacy—Study and teaching (Elementary)
    4. Electronic information resource literacy—Study and teaching (Elementary)—United States.
    I. Berkowitz, Robert E.   II. Title.   III. Title: Teaching information & technology skills.
    ZA3075.E42   1999
    372.3'58'044—dc21
                                                                               99-29894
                                                                                  CIP

Published by Linworth Publishing, Inc.
480 East Wilson Bridge Road, Suite L
Worthington, Ohio 43085

Series Information:
    From The Professional Growth Series

ISBN 0-938865-81-1

5 4 3 2 1

Table of Contents

Table of Contents continued

Table of Contents continued

Table of Figures

Table of Worksheets

Acknowledgements

Another book completed—our first for Linworth! It's very exciting. And, believe us, it doesn't get any easier! For us, writing a book takes a lot of hard work—and not just by us. There are many people who we must acknowledge and thank.

First, there are Barbara Jansen and Tami Little, who have contributed substantively to the content of this book. We are fortunate to have these highly creative (and busy) educators choose to share their expertise with us and with our readers.

Second, we are particularly grateful to Sue Wurster for marshalling the book through. Sue was a tireless manager and editor with a very difficult task—getting us to complete what we promised—in a timely fashion. She always did so in an encouraging and friendly (but firm) way. Sue also helped with editorial decisions, including determining structure and selecting entries. Sue deserves high praise for the quality of this final product.

Carrie Lowe also provided valuable assistance in completing sections of this book including the section on the Super3. Carrie, who currently works on the GEM project for the Information Institute of Syracuse, writes the "Big6 In Action: Reports from the Front Lines" column for *The Big6 Newsletter*.

We also wish to thank our many students and colleagues who encourage us to refine and share our Big6 approach. It's because of you that we continue to develop the Big6 and supporting materials. Thanks for your numerous and excellent ideas.

Our long-term friend and new publisher, Marlene Woo-Lun, deserves a special thank you and recognition. Marlene is one of the most up-beat and fun people we know. But, Marlene is also dead serious in her commitment and support of education and libraries. It is a pleasure to work in true collaboration with a publisher.

No one gives us more encouragement than our wives, Carol Eisenberg and Joyce Berkowitz, and our children, Brian; Laura; Adam; and Marette, who share our enthusiasm and are uncomplaining when our family time is taken by our work on the Big6.

Last, we wish to acknowledge each other in our various tasks in the partnership that results in our Big6 work and this book. Our investments in each other are deep, and we hope they are reflected in the fabric of this material.

Mike Eisenberg & Bob Berkowitz

In memory of Lenny Eisenberg, our teacher.

About the Authors

Michael B. Eisenberg is director and professor in the School of Library and Information Science, University of Washington (Seattle) and co-founder of AskERIC, the online question answering service for the K–12 community. His work focuses on the use of information and information technology by individuals and organizations to meet their information needs and manage their information more effectively and efficiently. Mike conducts research, writes, consults, and lectures frequently on information problem-solving, information technology, the Internet, and information management in learning and teaching.

Mike is a graduate of State University of New York at Albany (B.A. and M.L.S). He earned a certificate of advanced studies and a Ph.D. in information transfer from Syracuse University.

Robert E. Berkowitz is library media specialist at Wayne Central High School (Ontario Center, NY). Bob has successfully managed school libraries for Head Start–12th grade in both rural and urban settings. He has been an educational professional since 1971. Bob is a strong believer in active, curriculum-centered library media programs and promotes the integration of information literacy skills across the entire curriculum. He consults with state education departments, school districts, and local schools. He also shares his ideas at state, regional, and local conferences and seminars. Bob is an adjunct professor at Syracuse University's School of Information Studies and has taught at other institutions of higher education.

Bob is a graduate of the American International College, B.A. (Springfield, MA). He earned an M.A. in Education, George Washington University; M.L.S., State University of New York at Albany; and School Administrator's Certification, North Adams State College (North Adams, MA).

About the Contributors

Barbara A. Jansen is the library media specialist and campus technology facilitator at Forest Creek Elementary School (Round Rock, TX). She specializes in integrating information problem-solving skills, content area curriculum, and technology. She is also a part-time faculty member at the University of Texas at Austin Graduate School of Library and Information Science.

Barbara is a graduate of the University of Texas at Austin (B.S., M.Ed., M.L.I.S.).

Tami J. Little is a K–12 librarian and 2nd grade teacher. She is responsible for the information literacy curriculum in her building and coordinates the integration of technology in the classroom. Tami is an adjunct faculty member for Morningside College, Sioux City, Iowa and Wayne State College, Wayne, Nebraska.

Tami earned her B.A. and an M.A. in education from Morningside College, Sioux City, Iowa, and an M.L.S. degree from Emporia (Kansas) State University.

Foreword

The Big6™ Skills approach to information & technology skills instruction is a systematic process that continually grows in sophistication as learners grow and develop.

This book offers ideas that will enable school library media specialists and teachers to understand the Big6 approach and the rationale behind it. Specific techniques, strategies, and ways to build the Big6 Skills into existing instructional programs will be discussed, as well as ways to create new units and lessons.

This book includes specific sample Big6 instructional ideas in context that can be used as is or modified to meet specific instructional needs. These instructional ideas can provide the basis for developing a powerful information & technology skills instructional program.

Contributors to this volume are experienced school library media professionals. We provide detailed information to help you get started or to expand your existing Big6 program.

Our philosophy is that, in an information age, information & technology skills are basic education. We believe that library media specialists and other teachers need to encourage information-based, problem-solving, and decision-making skills that empower students and improve literacy.

We hope that Teaching Information & Technology Skills: The Big6™ in Elementary Schools *will be a major contribution to the field of information & technology skills instruction. Library media specialists and teachers using this book can change what happens in their library media centers, technology labs, and classrooms.*

PART 1

Overview of the Big6™ Approach

CHAPTER 1

Introduction: The Need

The Information Problem

It's almost a cliché to say that we live in an increasingly complex world, an information age. However, that doesn't make it any less true or any less difficult to manage. Here are some statistics that describe the information explosion that all of us face every day:

- More information has been produced in the last 30 years than in the previous 5,000 (Large, *The Micro Revolution, Revisited*, 1984).

- Science and technology information increases 13% each year and doubles every five and one-half years (Naisbitt, *Megatrends*, 1982).

- "According to a study by the Commerce Department, Internet traffic is doubling every hundred days," says Michael Rappa, Editor, *CyberScape Digest*, Faulker Information Services (4/17/98), and *USA Today* reported that the number of World Wide Web sites doubles every 40–50 days!

Information anxiety is rampant. People even get physically sick as a result of the stress caused by information overload. It's true, and it's even got its own medical term: Information Fatigue Syndrome (*Investor's Business Daily*, 1996). There's simply too much information being created, stored, processed, and presented.

By the time students enter high school, they are almost always reacting to information demands placed upon them by others.

Being overloaded is the norm; people just can't keep up. And we aren't just talking about people in the workforce or higher education. Even elementary students are having difficulties meeting the information demands.

Dr. Melissa Gross recently studied the information behaviors of school-age children. Dr. Gross (1998) looked at why students were searching for information, comparing self-driven questions and needs vs. questions and needs imposed by others—including teachers. Not surprisingly, she found that as students progress in school, they search less and less for their own purposes. More and more of their searching is in response to imposed needs. By the time students enter high school, they are almost always reacting to information demands placed upon them by others.

Gross' findings confirm our own observations concerning the reading habits of K–12 students. In the lower grades, students have more time to read for pleasure and take more time to read on their own. But, as they get older, students have less time for their own reading or to pursue their own interests. The demands imposed on them—the *information* demands—are substantial in terms of what they are asked to do as well as the difficulties of finding, processing, and presenting information.

Again, there's just too much "stuff" out there, and it's not easy to keep up. At the same time, there's an irony—yes, we are surrounded by information, but we can never seem to find what we want, when we want it, and in the form we want it.

One solution to the information problem— the one that seems to be most often adopted in schools (as well as in business and society in general)—is to speed things up. We try to pack in more and more content, to work faster to get more done. But, this is a losing proposition. It's like that old *I Love Lucy* show—the one with Lucy and Ethel on the candy factory line. The candy comes through on the conveyor belt, and Lucy and Ethel are to wrap each piece of candy. They start out fine, feeling pretty good and saying things like, "This is easy. We can handle this." But soon the candy is moving faster and faster. They start struggling, pulling the candy off the belt, stuffing the pieces under their hats, in their mouths, and in their uniforms while exclaiming, "We're fighting a losing game!"

In education too, speeding things up can only work for so long. Instead, we need to think about helping students to work smarter not faster. There is an alternative to speeding things up. It's the smarter solution, one that helps students develop the skills and understandings they need to find, process, and use information effectively. This smarter solution focuses on process as well as content. Some people call this smarter solution information literacy or information skills instruction. We call it the Big6.

The Big6 and Other Process Models

The Big6 is a process model of how people of all ages solve an information problem. From practice and study, we found that successful information problem-solving encompasses six stages:

- Task Definition
- Information Seeking Strategies

...Yes, we are surrounded by information, but we can never seem to find what we want, when we want it, and in the form we want it.

- Location & Access
- Use of Information
- Synthesis
- Evaluation

People go through these Big6 stages— consciously or not—when they seek or apply information to solve a problem or make a decision. It's not necessary to complete these stages in a linear order, and a given stage doesn't have to take a lot of time. We have found that in almost all successful problem-solving situations all stages are completed.

The Big6 shares some similarities with other process models. For example, one generic guide to improved problem-solving and creative thinking is Koberg and Bagnall's "Problem-Solving Feedback Perspective" from *The Universal Traveler* (1980). Theirs is a seven-step approach that begins by accepting the existing situation or problem and moves to analyzing the components of the problem, defining the problem, brainstorming, and selecting the solution, implementation, and evaluation. This model is characterized by its logical pattern that begins with understanding a problem exists and ends, not with implementing a solution, but rather an evaluation of the effects of the action taken. This allows for reassessment to determine if the problem or any aspects of the problem still exist.

A process model widely used in gifted and talented education is the "Creative Problem Solving" model (Noller, Parnes, and Biondi, 1976). The five major steps in this model are:

- Fact-finding: Collect all data surrounding the problem.

- Problem-finding: Restate the problem in a more solvable form.

- Idea-finding: Brainstorm and defer judgment in an attempt to develop as many ideas as possible for solving the problem.

- Solution-finding: Select the criteria for evaluating solutions, and then apply the criteria to each possible solution. Choose the best solution.

- Acceptance-finding: Present the solution to all parties involved to decide if it would be workable. Plan, implement, and evaluate the solution.

There are also a number of information literacy process models coming from the library media field: Stripling and Pitts (1988), Kuhlthau (1985, 1993), and Pappas and Tepe (1995), as well as the new national standards from the American Association of School Librarians and the Association of Educational Communications and Technology (1998). It is encouraging that there are more similarities among the models than differences. (See Appendix A, p. 137 for a comparison of information literacy models.) The driving force behind these models is "process"—that is, understanding that information skills are not isolated incidents but rather connected activities that encompass a way of thinking about and using information.

Teaching and Learning the Big6

In addition to considering the Big6 as a process, another useful way to view the Big6 is as a set of basic, essential life skills. These skills can be applied across situations—to school, personal, and work settings. The Big6 Skills are applicable to all subject areas across the full range of grade levels. Students use the Big6 Skills whenever they need information to solve a problem, make a decision, or complete a task.

The Big6 Skills are best learned when integrated with classroom curriculum and activities. Teachers can begin to use the Big6 immediately by:

- Using the Big6 terminology when giving various tasks and assignments

- Talking students through the process for a particular assignment

...Information skills are not isolated incidents, but rather connected activities that encompass a way of thinking about and using information.

- Asking key questions and focusing attention on specific Big6 actions to accomplish.

For example, suppose students are learning about animals. They may need to complete a worksheet or prepare a more extensive report. A teacher can state, "Task Definition—what are you trying to accomplish? What types and how much information will you need to do it?" The teacher can then go through the rest of the Big6—prompting students to ensure that they consider the various aspects of the full process in relation to the animals assignment. Later, teachers or library media specialists can provide specific lessons on more Big6 stages—at the relevant time as the students work on their animal project. Chapter 4 provides more detail on implementation of the Big6, and the second part of this book includes examples in context.

Beyond incorporating the Big6 into everyday classroom practice, we recommend that teachers work with library media specialists and technology teachers to systematically plan to teach the Big6 Skills as part of the curriculum. Learning these essential information skills takes effort and repetition. Students need opportunities to develop in-depth expertise in each of the Big6 Skills. This requires a planned program of instruction and learning. Again, see Chapter 4 for more information on implementing the Big6.

Various computer and information technology skills are integral parts of the Big6 Skills. For example, when students use word processing to write a letter, that's Big6 #5, Synthesis. When they search for information on the World Wide Web, that's Big6 #3, Location & Access. When they use e-mail to discuss an assignment with another student or the teacher, that's Big6 #1, Task Definition. Using computers can "turbo-boost" students' abilities.

Teaching and learning to use technology as part of the Big6 process is very helpful for students and teachers. Students see the connection between various technology skills and how the skills can be applied. Teachers have a context for integrating technology instruction into classroom learning, assignments, and projects. Instead of focusing on the technology itself, teachers can help students think about what they want to accomplish and how technology might help them reach their goals.

The Big6-technology connection is explored in Chapter 3. But first, it's time to focus on the Big6 process and skills in detail.

REFLECTIONS

The BIG 6

REFLECTIONS

CHAPTER 2

The Big6 Process and Skills

As explained in Chapter 1, the Big6 can be described both as a set of essential life skills and as a process. This is a strength of the Big6 approach—it provides a unified, process-context for learning and teaching information and technology skills.

We also find it's useful to explain the Big6 in a top-down fashion. That is, when working with children, we first try to have them understand that the Big6 is a process, from beginning to end. Then, we focus on the main six stages—from Task Definition to Evaluation. Finally, we have two sub-stages under each of the Big6. This results in twelve sub-stages, the "Little12." The Big6 is presented in more detail below in terms of these various levels of specificity.

The Big6 is applicable to every age group and level of development—from pre-K to senior citizen. For example, we present the idea of process and the Big6 to very young children with something called the "Super3." The three stages of the Super3 are: beginning, middle, and end, and it's an easy way to get young children to think about how they go about completing a task. We offer more about the Super3 at the end of this chapter, but first, we present a more complete explanation of the levels of the Big6.

Levels of the Big6

Level 1: The Conceptual Level

> *Whenever students are faced with an information-based problem to solve— e.g., homework, an assignment, test, quiz, or decision—they can use the Big6 approach.*

The broadest level of the Big6 approach is the conceptual or overview level. Here, we are trying to establish the concept of process and flow. Whether we realize it or not, we undertake a process with every assignment or information task. Recognizing the process and our personal preferences for problem-solving can help us be more effective and efficient. As part of this, at this broad level, we recommend helping students learn the following:

- To recognize that most problems have a strong information component; the problems are information-rich

- To recognize and identify the information aspects of that problem

- To realize that information-rich problems can be solved systematically and logically

- To understand that the Big6 Skills will help them solve the problem effectively and efficiently.

The Big6 Skills

1 📷 *Task Definition*

2 🔍 *Information Seeking Strategies*

3 🖱 *Location & Access*

4 👂 *Use of Information*

5 🧩 *Synthesis*

6 📋 *Evaluation*

Level 2: The Big6

The second level in the Big6 approach includes the set of six distinct skills that comprise the general problem-solving method: The Big6 Skills.

When students are in a situation that requires information problem-solving, they should use these skills, consciously or not. We have found that completing each of these six stages successfully is necessary for solving information problems. The stages do not necessarily need to be completed in order, nor are people always aware that they are engaging in a particular stage. However, at some point in time, children need to define the task; select, locate, and use appropriate information sources; pull the information together; and decide that the task is, in fact, complete.

Level 3: The Big6 Component Skills —The Little12

Each of the six major Big6 Skills can be subdivided into two sub-skills, or the "Little12." Through research, experience, and careful diagnosis, each of the six skills can be subdivided into two sub-skills, the "Little12." These component skills provide a more specific categorization of the general approach to problem solving and allow for the design and development of instruction.

Though there is no requirement that any of the Big6 components be addressed in any particular order, it is often useful to define the task before attempting to do anything else. After all, unless we know what we are expected to do, understand the nature and parameters of the problem, and can identify the information sources that will help us solve it, there is little chance for success. We would be remiss if we did not lead by example. The following sections will explain Task Definition in more detail and provide specific examples.

Components of the Big6 Skills

1 Task Definition
1.1 Define the problem.

1.2 Identify the information needed.

2 Information Seeking Strategies
2.1 Determine all possible sources.

2.2 Select the best sources.

3 Location & Access
3.1 Locate sources.

3.2 Find information within sources.

4 Use of Information
4.1 Engage (e.g., read, hear, view).

4.2 Extract relevant information.

5 Synthesis
5.1 Organize information from multiple sources.

5.2 Present the result.

6 Evaluation
6.1 Judge the result (effectiveness).

6.2 Judge the process (efficiency).

1 Task Definition

Task Definition refers to what students are trying to accomplish. The key to successful information problem-solving is to focus on the purpose and need for information.

> **Task Definition:**
> **1.1 Define the problem.**
> **1.2 Identify the information needed.**

1.1 Define the problem.

What is the problem to be solved? This is the initial question that students must consider and answer. Students often start with a fuzzy sense of what is being asked of them. They need to learn how to think about the full scope of the task and then narrow their focus. How the information problem is initially defined will determine the kinds of solutions or decisions to be considered throughout the process.

Examples of Task Definition 1.1:

- Students demonstrate the ability to determine what is required in an assignment.

- Students demonstrate the ability to know that information is needed to complete the assignment.

- Students demonstrate the ability to select, narrow, or broaden topics.

- Students demonstrate the ability to formulate questions based on topics and subtopics.

1.2 Identify the information needed.

What types of information are needed in order to solve the problem or make the decision? Before turning to specific information sources, students should consider whether they need facts or opinions (or both) and primary or secondary sources. They should also consider the amount of information needed—a single source, a few resources, or as fully comprehensive as possible. Lastly, they should consider the desired formats—text, graphics, audio, or video.

Examples of Task Definition 1.2:

- Students demonstrate the ability to pick out key words embedded in a question or assignment.

- Students demonstrate the ability to recognize that the homework assignment requires factual information from at least three library sources.

- Students demonstrate the ability to determine statements that require evidence for support.

- Students demonstrate the ability to recognize the need to gather information from people through the use of an interview, survey, or questionnaire.

Task Definition is the stage at which students determine what needs to be done and what information is needed to get the job done. We find that the number one problem situation students have is not realizing what's really expected of them. There are many reasons for this (the student may not have been paying attention, the task is difficult or confusing, the teacher was not completely clear). Regardless of the reason, students are at a tremendous disadvantage if they don't understand what they are required to do as well as the basis for grading.

Teachers can help with Task Definition by bringing the task and the criteria for assessment and grading into focus. Look at assignments—are all parts included and clear? Do the students truly understand? If not, we need to find ways to ensure that students comprehend and focus. Most often, teachers give some form of direction concerning an assignment. They write the instructions on the board, discuss assignments, or give out some form of handout. These are useful approaches; however, these forms of communication about the task are mostly one-way and informational (making sure students have the information) rather than instructional (helping students learn how to define tasks, zero in on critical aspects, and determine how they will fulfill the assignment at an appropriate level). Explaining an assignment is about as far as most teachers go. The assumption is that students will then know what to do and how to do it. Right? Wrong! Don't assume anything! We've frequently found that students in the intermediate and higher grades really don't understand what is meant by such aspects of assignments as:

- Compare and contrast
- Cite your sources
- Summarize
- Choose among
- Outline
- Describe.

In teaching Task Definition, we can use subject area assignments to help students learn effective and efficient ways to size up a task, understand what is being asked of them, and determine the nature and types of information they need in order to complete the task.

One way to do this is to give students an assignment along with two or three samples of completed work. Be sure to include at least one very poor sample, virtually a parody of the assignment. Have the students assess the samples in terms of the assignment:

- Does it do what was required?
- Is it complete?
- How could it be improved?

Another technique is to purposely give almost no direction on an assignment. Teachers often lead students through every step in an assignment—verbally or in writing. Sometimes it is necessary for teachers to be very directive and specific, but too often this is done without even thinking of the message

being communicated. When teachers give a great deal of detail or step-by-step directions, *they* are doing most of the Task Definition work. The teachers are assuming primary responsibility understanding and defining the specifics of assignments.

We want students to assume ownership and responsibility for assignments. Therefore, try giving almost no detail about a project, homework assignment, or quiz. Set aside time to answer any and all questions about the assignment, but put the burden on the students to find out exactly what is expected.

When working with children, we encourage them to do "brain surgery" on their teachers—without actually opening up the skull! Students need to get inside their teacher's head—to figure out exactly what the teacher has in mind—because the students will suffer the consequences if they don't. Again, the goal is to move the responsibility for Task Definition from teacher to student.

The second part to Task Definition (1.2) calls for identifying the information needed and determining the information requirements of an assignment. Here, we're not talking about various sources (books, computer databases, and magazines). The sources come later. In 1.2, we want students to think about what types of information they will need to get the job done (facts, opinions, pictures, and numerical information) and about how much information they will need.

The type of information problem and the way students define the task will suggest to them the kinds of information they will need. This in turn will suggest to students how they can find the information. This is an exercise "in gathering" all possible sources and sorting and selecting the best sources for the task at hand. This next section will describe the Big6 stage of "Information Seeking Strategies" and offer examples of how this stage furthers the information problem-solving process.

❷ Information Seeking Strategies

Information Seeking Strategies refer to determining the alternative information sources available that are appropriate to the information need. It's a mind-expanding stage that encourages students to think broadly and creatively.

> **Information Seeking Strategies:**
> **2.1 Determine all possible sources.**
> **2.2 Select the best sources.**

2.1 Determine all possible sources.

What are all possible sources of information? Determining the universe of information sources appropriate to solving the information problem is an essential step after clarifying the task at hand. Knowledge of sources as well as imagination and creativity are important in successfully completing the step of determining likely sources.

Examples of Information Strategies 2.1:

■ Students demonstrate the ability to generate a list of potential information sources, text and human, for a given information problem.

■ Students demonstrate the ability to determine that an experiment is the appropriate way to gather information for a question about ecology.

■ Students demonstrate the ability to recognize the Internet as a valuable resource.

■ Students demonstrate the ability to ask the library media specialist if there are any good Web sources for information about space exploration.

■ Students demonstrate the ability to identify electronic sources (e.g., CD-ROM, online databases).

2.2 Select the best sources.

What are the best possible information sources—in a particular situation and at a certain point in time? This is the key question in 2.2. It is not only important to determine the range of sources, but it is also vital to examine the sources in order to select those that are most likely to provide quality information to meet the task as defined.

Examples of Information Strategies 2.2:

■ Students demonstrate the ability to decide that the National Geographic CD-ROM is the perfect source to complete the homework assignment.

■ Students demonstrate the ability to decide that a segment from a current PBS program is a better source of information about whales than a magazine article from ten years ago.

■ Students demonstrate the ability to assess the value of online discussion groups in relation to their task.

■ Students demonstrate the ability to select sources that are suitable to meet the information need (e.g., current, authoritative, understandable, useful, available).

Once students understand the task or problem and have some idea about the types of information needed, their attention must turn to the range of possible information sources. This is the stage when students examine the possible information sources and then select the sources that are most appropriate and available. Once they get into it, kids are generally quite good at brainstorming sources. The goal is to get them to think broadly.

For example, when starting a report or project, students tend to rely on the usual sources—books, reference materials, and magazines. There are other sources that they generally overlook. These neglected sources include local and regional topic experts, historical societies, computer sources, and documentary films. Students might greatly enhance their projects by consulting these sources. Students must first think broadly about all types of sources. They must then narrow and select those sources that really meet their needs in terms of richness of information and availability. Brainstorm and narrow—these are critical thinking skills that can be developed with children of all ages.

Teachers can help by building into their classroom various brainstorming activities to identify the wide range of possible sources. For example, break the students into small groups and have each group brainstorm and narrow related to a topic, then compare results with the whole class. Or, present an assignment and a list of possible sources. Then, on a card, have each student write down their source of choice and their reason for selecting that source.

Identifying the range of all possible sources and even selecting the best sources can be fun, but it is not very helpful for solving a problem unless the students are able to actually retrieve the information they need. The Big6 recognizes this dilemma by requiring that students have the skills to locate and access information. That's the next stage of the Big6.

3 Location & Access

Location & Access refer to finding and retrieving information sources as well as specific information within sources.

> **Location & Access:**
> **3.1 Locate sources.**
> **3.2 Find information within sources.**

3.1 Locate sources.

This is the stage where students find the sources physically or electronically. They need to determine where the sources are located—in the classroom, library, or some other place? How are the sources organized in those places—alphabetically by topic or author, by the Dewey Decimal classification system, not at all? Are there electronic tools for access such as an online catalog, or is the information itself available on the Web or some other electronic format? And, if the source is a person, can they be reached by telephone or e-mail, or is it best (or necessary) to meet them in person?

Examples of Location & Access 3.1:

- Students demonstrate the ability to locate sources in the library.
- Students demonstrate the ability to use a search engine on the Internet.
- Students demonstrate the ability find sources by Dewey Decimal number.
- Students demonstrate the ability to find the ABC books in their classroom.
- Students demonstrate the ability to arrange to interview a community member.

3.2 Find information within sources.

This stage refers to actually getting to the information in a given source. Once the source is located, students must find the specific information they need. This isn't the most glamorous of skills, but it is essential nevertheless. And, there is a key to this stage—it's learning to search for and then use—the INDEX! This is the librarian's secret weapon—the index. Librarians and teachers have traditionally taught students about indexes, but doing so within the Big6 process makes a lot more sense to children.

Examples of Location & Access 3.2:

- Students demonstrate the ability to use the index in their textbook.

- Students demonstrate the ability to use a table of contents.

- Students demonstrate the ability to look up locations on a map.

- Students use a search tool in an electronic encyclopedia to get to the needed section.

- Students demonstrate the ability to skim to find the appropriate material on a Web site.

Location & Access should be the easiest stage, but it often isn't. It's also not a very exciting or particularly interesting stage. But, it does need to be completed if your children are to succeed. The goal in this stage is to locate the sources selected under the Information Seeking Strategies stage and then actually get to the information in those sources. In the past, librarians and teachers spent a great deal of time on this part of the process. That's changing because they realize that Location & Access is only part of the overall process.

Again, a crucial tool that can save lots of time in Location & Access of sources is an index. Indexes of various kinds (Yellow Pages, directories in shopping malls, back-of-the-book indexes, online magazine databases) make it easier to find information. Indexes may not be exciting, but they really do save time and effort. Kids should always be on the lookout for indexes and they should know how to use them. Of course, indexes aren't the only way to locate and access information. Sometimes we just browse through the shelves, skim a book, or surf the Internet!

Teachers can help their students with Location & Access in lots of ways. For example, they can help in math by teaching how to search the textbook or class notes for examples of how to solve a type of problem. Or, they can demonstrate by example using a back-of-the-book index while the children watch. Just recognizing "indexes" is a valuable lesson. Have students keep a log for one week of every time they used an index—what, why, how, and how useful was it?

Locating sources and accessing the appropriate sections within sources completes an important stage of the information problem-solving process. The students have gathered at least some of the necessary sources to complete their tasks. Now, they must focus their attention even more—by engaging the information within the sources and extracting what's really relevant. This requires critical thinking in terms of reading and other forms of processing information and making decisions about the value of information in terms of being on target, useful, current, and accurate. That's the next stage—#4, Use of Information.

4 Use of Information

Use of Information refers to the application of information to meet defined information tasks.

> **Use of Information**
> **4.1 Engage (e.g., read, hear, view).**
> **4.2 Extract relevant information.**

4.1 Engage (e.g., read, hear, view).

What information does the source provide? Ultimately, to gain useful and meaningful information from a source requires students to read, listen, or view in some form. We call these processes "engaging" the information, and it is crucially important. The widespread emphasis on reading and its role in overall achievement attests to the importance of this stage.

> **Examples of Use of Information 4.1:**
>
> ■ Students demonstrate the ability to listen attentively to directions.
>
> ■ Students demonstrate the ability to watch a weather report for local storm conditions.
>
> ■ Students demonstrate the ability to interview a community helper for a 2nd grade project.
>
> ■ Students demonstrate the ability to read a topographic map.
>
> ■ Students demonstrate the ability to interact with a Web site.

4.2 Extract relevant information.

What specific information is worth applying to the task? This is determining "relevance" and can only be determined when students read, listen, or watch effectively. Even when students do locate sources and find appropriate information, they must be able to read and understand, listen effectively, or watch for key concepts and examples relevant to their task. Otherwise, the source will not help them meet their information need. Extraction also involves taking the information

with you in some way. This can include note-taking, copying and pasting, downloading, filming or recording, or sometimes just remembering.

> **Examples of Use of Information 4.2:**
>
> ■ Students demonstrate the ability to take notes while viewing a video tape in a social studies class about Native American traditions.
>
> ■ Students demonstrate the ability to underline or highlight the topic statement from an article on the migration of salmon.
>
> ■ Students demonstrate the ability to trace an outline of a state map from an encyclopedia article.
>
> ■ Students demonstrate the ability to cut and paste information from an electronic source into a word processing document.
>
> ■ Students demonstrate the ability to properly cite information sources.

Locating and accessing information is easy compared to actually making use of the information found in the sources. This usually requires the child to: read, view, or listen; decide what's important for the particular task at hand; and finally extract the needed information. This isn't always easy to do and could certainly take a considerable amount of time.

Teachers already do a great deal in this stage. Lessons and exercises on reading, viewing, or listening for a purpose, comprehension, and note-taking all help students to develop their Use of Information skills. Connecting these activities to the Big6 process can reinforce the role of these skills in the overall problem-solving process. Teachers and librarians can also focus various ways to skim or scan—in print or electronically—and then how to "capture" that information for use in their own work. Online databases, digital and video cameras, cassette recorders, and other technological tools provide new means for students to capture and use information. And yes, there is the potential for misrepresenting work as their own, so students must be helped to learn the necessity and ways of properly crediting authors and sources from all types of formats.

Putting a project together or completing an assignment is a lot like baking a cake—once all the separate ingredients are identified, extraneous items put aside, and the relevant ingredients ordered and handled correctly, they need to be combined.

Synthesis is the fifth stage of the Big6. This is the point when students pull together the information and begin to create the final project. Today, we have powerful new technology tools for Synthesis— from word processing to desktop publishing to multimedia and Web authoring. Therefore, Synthesis includes instruction on using these tools while at the same time going beyond the glitz to focus on developing good techniques and skills for organizing and presenting information in writing, graphic, and oral forms.

5 Synthesis

Synthesis refers to the integration and presentation of information from a variety of sources to meet the information need as defined.

> **Synthesis:**
> **5.1 Organize information from multiple sources.**
> **5.2 Present the result.**

5.1 Organize information from multiple sources.

The key question in Synthesis is "How does the information from all of the sources fit together?" This skill focuses on determining the best ways to pull together, integrate, and organize the information to meet the task.

Examples of Synthesis 5.1:

- Students demonstrate the ability to combine information from a newspaper article and notes collected from interviews with six students about a current events issue.

- Students demonstrate the ability to put dates and events in the right order on a timeline.

- Students demonstrate the ability to organize pictures so that they make sense.

- Students demonstrate the ability to prepare a sketch for a diorama of one Civil War battle.

- Students demonstrate the ability to use word processing or multimedia presentation software to arrange information.

5.2 Present the result.

How is the information best presented? What are the choices for presentation (e.g., written, graphic, oral, and multimedia), and how are those choices completed?

Examples of Synthesis 5.2:

- Students demonstrate the ability to use graphics in a speech.

- Students demonstrate the ability to represent a still life in different media.

- Students demonstrate the ability to use *PowerPoint* to create electronic slide shows.

- Students demonstrate the ability to draw and label a map of Africa.

- Students demonstrate the ability to use electronic spreadsheets or other tools to graph data collected during a science experiment.

- Students demonstrate the ability to properly cite electronic sources of information in bibliographies.

Synthesis involves organizing and presenting the information—putting it all together to finish the job. Sometimes Synthesis can be as simple as relaying a specific fact (as in answering a short-answer question) or making a decision (deciding on a topic for a report, a product to buy, an activity to join). At other times, Synthesis can be very complex and can involve the use of several sources, a variety of media or presentation formats, and the effective communication of abstract ideas.

Computer applications can help students organize and present information. Word processing, graphics programs, desktop publishing, databases, spreadsheets, and presentation packages can all help students put information together and present it effectively.

Teachers don't have to be experts with any of these tools in order to help students learn to use them effectively. Teachers can arrange for librarians, technology teachers, or even expert students to help students learn the capabilities and features of a program. But, the important aspects are still the same regardless of tool or format:

■ Using information to draw conclusions
■ Forming judgments based on evidence
■ Creating a logical argument
■ Organizing and communicating in a way that makes sense
■ Drawing conclusions
■ Presenting a coherent whole.

Throughout the information problem-solving process, students should reflect on where they are and how they are doing. Students need to figure out where they are in the project or assignment, whether they are making progress toward its completion, how good it is, and how well they are using the available time. This is Evaluation, Big6 stage #6. But Evaluation is not meant to just be the final action that students take—a summary at the end. Evaluation is an activity that students need to get in the habit of doing all the time.

6 Evaluation

In the Big6 process, evaluation refers to judgments on two different matters: (1) the degree to which the information problem is solved and (2) the information problem-solving process itself.

> **Evaluation:**
> **6.1 Judge the result (effectiveness).**
> **6.2 Judge the process (efficiency).**

6.1 Judge the result (effectiveness).

Was the problem solved? This is one concern in Evaluation. While working on an assignment, students can assess whether they are making progress on completing the task as defined. Sometimes they realize that they don't quite understand the task or that they need to go back and change or adjust the task. Upon completion, the students must ultimately recognize when the information problem has been solved and the quality of the result—hopefully in comparison to clearly stated criteria for judging quality.

Examples of Evaluation 6.1:

■ Students demonstrate the ability to evaluate multimedia presentations for both content and format.

■ Students demonstrate the ability to determine whether they are on the right track in their science experiment.

■ Students demonstrate the ability to judge the effectiveness of three different TV commercials.

■ Students demonstrate the ability to rate their projects based on a predetermined set of criteria.

6.2 Judge the process (efficiency).

For students to continue to improve their Big6 Skills, they need to learn how to assess their abilities. They should also consider what they can do to be more efficient in carrying out each component skill.

- Students demonstrate the ability to assess their confidence in answering a question about the structure and function of the human heart.

- Students demonstrate the ability to thoughtfully consider how well they were able to use electronic sources throughout their project.

- Students demonstrate the ability to talk about what was most difficult in completing an assignment.

- Students demonstrate the ability to compare the amount of time spent thinking about an art project and the amount of time actually working on the same art project.

- Students demonstrate the ability to reflect on their level of personal effort and time spent during their work on the assignment.

In the Evaluation stage, students should reflect on the result and the process of their work. Are they pleased with what they are doing or have completed? If they could do the project again, what might they do differently? Evaluation determines the effectiveness and efficiency of the information problem-solving process. Effectiveness is another way of saying, how good is the product? What grade are you likely to get? Efficiency refers to time and effort. If the children were to do the work again, how could they do as well, but save some time and effort?

Even young children can reflect on their performance. They look at their assignments, projects, and exams and decide if they are pleased with their result. It's not always necessary to get a top grade to be considered a success. Sometimes success is gaining a sense of accomplishment,

learning something totally new and different, or even just making an effort. Sometimes feeling "okay" is enough. At other times, students may want to strive for the very top performance as measured by grades. It helps to have kids understand and recognize the difference.

Students should also think about the process of completing tasks and assignments. Where did they get stuck or have difficulty? Where did they waste time? The point is to reflect on the process so they can make changes the next time. These kinds of self-reflections are valuable learning experiences.

Teachers need to develop techniques to get students involved in Evaluation. For example, set up "time-out" reflection points at various times while students are working on an assignment. Students can stop to confirm that they are clear about the assignment, assess their overall progress, and discuss any particular difficulties. Another technique is to have students keep a log and use it after the assignment is completed to discuss steps taken, successes, and areas for improvement.

Teachers should also provide clear directions and criteria for assessment. This doesn't mean being over-detailed or elaborate. It means making sure that students understand what they are being asked to do and how they will be graded. Scoring guides or rubrics are valuable tools for focusing attention on assessment. Ultimately, evaluation should encourage students to improve and help them to do so. Library media specialists can help by working with students on identifying what was the most difficult aspect of an assignment and what they might do differently next time.

Evaluation is the culmination of the entire Big6 process, but it is often the part of the process that receives the least attention. This is unfortunate because activities and exercises that emphasize Evaluation can actually help students in every Big6 stage as students reflect on their specific and overall strengths and skills.

The Super3

As explained at the beginning of this chapter, with very young children, we don't always start with explaining the full Big6 process. Instead, when we work with pre-school, kindergarten, and sometimes even first grade students, we present . . . the "Super3."

> - **BEGINNING Plan what you are going to do.**
> - **MIDDLE Do it.**
> - **END Review what you did.**

Beginning – Plan

In the beginning, when students receive an assignment or homework, they should first think:

- What am I supposed to do?
- What will the result look like if I do a really good job?
- What do I need to find out about in order to do the job?

Middle – Do

In the middle, students complete the various activities. This includes finding the necessary sources, reading or viewing the information in the sources, and putting it all together as a finished assignment.

End – Review

Finally, before the assignment is completely finished and turned in, students should again stop and think:

- Is this done?
- Did I do what I was supposed to do?
- Do I feel OK about this?
- Should I do something else before I turn it in?

That's the Super3, and it's easy for young children to remember and relate to. The Super3 emphasizes that children go through a process to get things done—just like characters in a story. We like to tell young children that when they are working on an assignment, they are the main character in a story. There are a number of techniques to get children started in thinking Super3:

- Share a story or two with the children and ask them to identify each of the Super3 elements in the story: what was the beginning, middle, and end?
- Give the students an assignment and ask them what they are supposed to do. See if they can make up a story about how a character would complete the assignment.
- Supply a story sheet that outlines a story according to the Super3. But leave out some key points, related to information needed in the story, to discuss with students.

The point is to use the story approach and be creative. Students are very open to thinking about themselves in relation to the Super3. We've seen some teachers have students make a storybook about themselves or produce a class book of Super3 stories.

In terms of helping students learn about the Super3, teachers of young children can teach and troubleshoot at each phase of the Super3 process. For example, for some children, beginning a project is the hardest thing to do. They may understand what they have to do, but have no idea what is the ultimate goal. Therefore, in the BEGINNING stage (Plan) include discussing what a finished product will look like. Later, you can help them brainstorm and choose possible sources for information.

Some children will start a project with gusto but later lose sight of the ultimate task. They simply cannot get the job done. These students are having trouble with the MIDDLE stage. To help trouble-shoot problems in the Middle, ask your children to explain what they have done up to that point. Have they lost sight of their goal? Are they stuck in one particular place? Once you help them get back on track, they can also think about what still lies ahead.

Lastly, at the END, children need to be able to tell whether they did a good job or not. We encourage students to estimate their success (sometimes as grades) before handing in a project or assignment. You can also use the story approach here. Ask them to tell you what they did in the form of a story. Then ask, "if you could do it again, what would you do differently? How could you make it better?" They don't actually need to go back and do it again. Recognizing how we would change things is all part of the learning process.

Summary

This chapter offered an extensive view of the Big6 process and the specifics of the Big6 Skills. The next chapter directly addresses the issue of technology for information problem-solving. Considering technology and technology tools within the Big6 process provides students with a powerful context for becoming effective and efficient users of information.

REFLECTIONS

REFLECTIONS

CHAPTER 3

Technology with a Big6 Face

Introduction

There seems to be clear and widespread agreement among educators, as well as in the general public, that students need to be proficient computer users—students need to be "computer literate." Furthermore, there is a growing awareness that being computer literate is more than simply being able to operate a computer. Students need to be able to use computers for a purpose.

We want students to know more than a particular set of commands or even how to use a particular type of software. We want students to use technology flexibly and creatively. We want them to be able to size up a task, recognize how technology might help them fulfill the task, and then use the technology to do so.

Helping students learn to apply technology in these ways requires a change in the way computer skills are traditionally taught in school. It means moving from teaching isolated "computer skills" to teaching integrated information and technology skills. For us, that means integrating computer skills within the Big6 problem-solving process. Individual computer skills take on a new meaning when they are integrated within the Big6, and students develop true "computer literacy" because they have

It means moving from teaching isolated "computer skills" to teaching integrated information and technology skills.

genuinely applied various computer and technology skills as part of the learning process.

Moving from teaching isolated computer skills to helping students learn integrated information and technology skills is not just a good idea—it's essential if we are to put students in a position to succeed in an increasingly complex and changing world. Peter Drucker, well-known management guru, stated that "executives have become computer-literate . . . but not many executives are information literate" (*Wall Street Journal*, Dec. 1, 1992, p.A16). Drucker is saying that being able to use computers is not enough. Executives must be able to apply computer skills to real situations and needs. Executives must be able to identify information problems and be able to locate, use, synthesize, and evaluate information in relation to those problems. These same needs exist for all people living in an information society.

There are many good reasons for moving from teaching isolated computer skills to teaching integrated information and technology skills. Technology is changing at a breath-taking pace and will continue to do so for the foreseeable future. In a speech at the 1997 National Educational Computing Conference in Seattle, Bill Gates recently stated that computing power has increased 1 million times over the past 20 years and will likely do so again in the next 20 years!

A million times more powerful. Will learning isolated specific skills such as keyboarding, word processing, and even World Wide Web searching suffice? Clearly not. Will learning to use whatever technologies come along to boost our skills within the overall information problem-solving process suffice? Absolutely.

That's what it means to look at technology from a Big6 perspective, to give technology a Big6 face.

Technology and the Big6

It's actually relatively easy to view technology from a Big6 perspective.

Let's take a typical basic technology— "a pencil and paper." In Big6 terms, how can a pencil and paper help us be more productive? Clearly, a pencil and paper boosts our ability to synthesize, organize, and present information, Big6 #5.

What are the electronic equivalents of a pencil and paper—the tools that help us even more to synthesize? Clearly, there's word processing. There's also desktop publishing, word processing,

HyperStudio, PowerPoint, and other presentation software programs. All these are used to organize and present information, Big6 #5.

Here's another basic technology—"a phone book." The phone book is an aid for Big6 #3–Location & Access. Electronic equivalents to the phone book? There are the online or CD-ROM bibliographic databases, Web browsers, and search engines (e.g., Yahoo!, Lycos, INFOSeek).

Other technologies can be viewed in this way. Similar to books, full-text databases, CD-ROM encyclopedias, and other electronic resources are part of an effective Information Seeking Strategy (Big6 #2) and are read/viewed/listened-to for information (Big6 #4). When a face-to-face meeting isn't possible, e-mail is highly useful for linking students with their teachers or with other students for Task Definition activities (Big6 #1) and later for Evaluation (Big6 #6). And more and more students are learning to take notes and extract information by using the copy and paste functions in word processing software.

When integrated into the information problem-solving process, these technological capabilities become powerful information tools for students. Figure 3.1 provides a summary of how some of today's technologies fit within the Big6 process.

Figure 3.1: Computer Capabilities and the Big6

Word processing	SYNTHESIS (writing) USE of INFORMATION (note-taking)
Spell/grammar checking	EVALUATION
Desktop publishing	SYNTHESIS
Presentation/Multimedia software	SYNTHESIS
Electronic spreadsheets	SYNTHESIS
Online library catalog	LOCATION & ACCESS
Electronic magazine index	LOCATION & ACCESS USE OF INFORMATION
Full-text electronic resources	INFORMATION SEEKING STRATEGIES USE OF INFORMATION
Brainstorming software	TASK DEFINITION
Copy-paste (in various programs)	USE OF INFORMATION

© 1987 Eisenberg & Berkowitz. Published by Linworth Publishing, Inc.

Examples of Technology in Big6 Contexts

Integrating technology instruction with the Big6 provides a context for technology skills instruction. It also helps students learn to apply technology flexibly and creatively.

In Chapter 4, we explain the importance of two contexts—the Big6 process and the classroom curriculum—to effective Big6 Skills instruction. This is particularly true for teaching technology skills. We avoid teaching technology skills in isolation when we combine them with the Big6 process and with real subject area curriculum and assignments.

For example, a 5th grade class is studying regions of the United States and comparing various features (e.g., geography, population, industry, and special attributes). The assignment is to create a comparative chart that highlights differences and similarities.

As students go through the work for the assignment, they engage in various stages of the Big6. The teacher recognizes that this might be a good opportunity to teach technology and the Big6. She arranges with the library media specialist for the students to learn about electronic searching for books in various electronic resources (Big6 #3, Location & Access). The students will also search on the World Wide Web and compare what they found in terms of quality, amount of information, and time and effort.

The teacher also speaks to the technology teacher about possible programs to help the students create charts (Big6 #5, Synthesis). The technology teacher recommends a draw/paint program and schedules the class for a special lesson.

This is a powerful example of the integration of technology, the Big6, and curriculum. Students are learning to use technology as part of the information problem-solving process to perform better in classroom curriculum.

> *Students are learning to use technology as part of the information problem-solving process to perform better in classroom curriculum.*

Another class is studying endangered species. Working in groups, the students are to create a formal report on the status of one type of animal. The students brainstorm possible sources and one group decides that talking to someone at the zoo would be a good idea (Big6 #2, Information Seeking Strategies). However, they realize they have no way of getting to the zoo (Big6 #3, Location & Access). Their teacher suggests they send an electronic message or e-mail to the library media specialist asking what to do. They do so, and she suggests conducting the interview through the Internet, either by e-mail or chat.

But, where can they find the zoo on the Web and the e-mail address of someone at the zoo (Big6 #3, Location & Access)? The students realize they can use a Web search engine to locate the local zoo website or other zoo websites, which probably include lists of staff. The library media specialist also e-mails to the students suggesting that if they get stuck, they can send e-mail to KidsConnect, a question-answering service on the Internet for kids (*AskKC@ala.org*).

Over the next few days, the students make contact with a local zoo employee who agrees to answer their questions via e-mail. The students e-mail the questions and are excited when they get a response in three days. They copy and paste from the e-mail into a word processing document and note the name of their contact, e-mail address, and dates of the e-mail exchanges.

Technologies incorporated in this example include the use of a messaging or e-mail program, Web search engine, Web browser, and word processing program. The copy-paste function from e-mail is also an important skill for the students to learn. Another twist to this assignment would be to use multi-media presentation software to create and present the report instead of a straight written format (Big6 Skill #5—Synthesis).

When we reflect on integrating technology skills into teaching and learning, we realize that it is not necessary to change the fundamentals of quality instruction or the information problem-solving perspective that is at the heart of the Big6 Skills approach. The implementation of technology through the Big6:

- Develops students' problem-solving, complex thinking, and information management abilities

- Enables students to become comfortable with technology and understand that the technologies are valuable tools to help them perform their work

- Focuses students' attention on using technologies as tools to extend knowledge and to individualize learning

- Develops an active participatory learning process in which students become self-directed learners

- Facilitates integrating technology across all grades and into all disciplines

- Assists teachers in changing their roles from presenters of information to learning coaches who offer tools and advice

- Helps teachers to introduce and have students use technologies even if the teachers aren't experts themselves.

Implementing technology within the Big6 process is easy, direct, and powerful. It also encourages classroom teachers, library media specialists, and technology teachers to collaboratively design instruction that can intentionally create challenging and exciting learning experiences. Such opportunities expand the scope of new technology use by all students.

The Big6 and the Internet

The Internet—particularly the World Wide Web—is an overwhelming technology that deserves special note. We constantly hear from teachers and students about there being so much information on the Web, but also that it's so hard to find what you want on the Web. How do you make sense of it all? How do you really use it effectively and efficiently?

Again, we fall back on the Big6 process. To make sense of the Web involves most of the Big6

Figure 3.2: Internet Capabilities and the Big6

E-mail, chat, messaging (ICQ)	TASK DEFINITION INFORMATION SEEKING STRATEGIES LOCATION & ACCESS USE OF INFORMATION SYNTHESIS EVALUATION
Mailing lists (listservs), newsgroups, chat,	TASK DEFINITION INFORMATION SEEKING STRATEGIES LOCATION & ACCESS USE OF INFORMATION SYNTHESIS EVALUATION
Web browsers (Netscape, Internet Explorer)	INFORMATION SEEKING STRATEGIES LOCATION & ACCESS
Search engines (Yahoo!, Hotbot, Lycos, Excite, Alta Vista)	INFORMATION SEEKING STRATEGIES LOCATION & ACCESS
Portals (My Yahoo!, MSN, AOL)	INFORMATION SEEKING STRATEGIES LOCATION & ACCESS USE OF INFORMATION
Web authoring (HTML)	SYNTHESIS
Websites	USE OF INFORMATION

process—from Task Definition to Evaluation. In the endangered animals example above, the students were able to use the Web to find zoo contacts. The Web is also rich in information about animals, and the students would probably use search tools and relevant websites as well. Figure 3.2 shows how Internet and Web capabilities fit within the Big6 context. All stages of the Big6 can benefit from use of the Internet and Web.

Here are some Big6 suggestions for using the Web in teaching:

Task Definition—Don't start with the Web; start with the problem. Discuss what the students are trying to accomplish and what the result might look like.

Information Seeking Strategies—Consider options and alternatives—even within the Web. Big6 #2.1 involves determining possibilities, #2.2 is to choose the best sources given the situation. That means applying criteria, such as closeness to the problem, accuracy, currency, and authority of each website. Students should be able to explain why they chose to use a particular website based on one or more of these criteria.

Location & Access—Search tools are a key! Discuss how the various search systems differ. Students should be able to explain why

they prefer one over another.

Use of Information—This stage involves selecting good information, again based on applying criteria. Discuss criteria and how to make choices based on criteria.

Synthesis—Ease-of-use is the primary concern in Synthesis. How easy is it to find information on a website? Is it logical, easy-to-understand, and simple to navigate?

Evaluation—One aspect to focus on is efficiency—saving time and effort while maintaining quality. This relates directly to the original concern of not being overwhelmed by information. What are some strategies for using the Web for a purpose but doing so without wasting considerable time?

We cannot overemphasize that the key for classroom, library, and technology teachers is not to focus on the Web or technology itself. We should focus on the learning goals, the content, and the Big6 process and then make the technology connection. For example, helping students become discriminating users of information—applying good judgment in selecting sources and information within sources—is central to the Big6 stages of Information Seeking Strategies and Use of

Figure 3.3: **The Big6 and Technology**

TASK DEFINITION	e-mail, group discussions (listservs, newsgroups), brainstorming software, chat (IRC, MOO, Palace), videoconferencing (CUSeeMe), groupware
INFO SEEKING STRATEGIES	online catalogs, info retrieval, electronic resources (CD-ROMs, intranet), WWW/net resources, AskERIC, KidsConnect, online discussion groups (listservs)
LOCATION & ACCESS	online catalogs, electronic indexes, WWW browers (Netscape, Internet Explorer), search engines (Yahoo, Alta Vista, Lycos, Hotbot), AskERIC, KidsConnect, telnet, ftp, e-mail
USE OF INFORMATION	upload/download, word processing, copy-paste, outliners, spreadsheets, databases (for analysis of data), statistical packages
SYNTHESIS	word processing, desktop publishing, graphics, spreadsheets, database management, hypermedia, presentation software, down/up load, ftp, e-journals, listservs, newsgroups, Web/HTML authoring
EVALUATION	spell/grammar checkers, e-mail, online discussions (listservs, newsgroups), chat (IRC, MOO, Palace), videoconferencing (CUSeeMe), groupware

Information. These essentials are transferable, long-term Big6 abilities. The way to help students gain these abilities is through integrating subject area—Big6—technology instruction.

Summary

This chapter provided a conceptual framework and approach for helping students learn and use technology in meaningful ways. Technologies can boost students' abilities to solve curriculum-based information problems. The key is to use technology within the Big6 process. Figure 3.3 presents the Big6 view and how various current technologies fit into the Big6.

The next chapter turns to the question of implementation. Teaching the Big6 and Web skills in context means determining when students actually are working on a project or assignment that lends itself to using the Web. Also, it's not necessary to cover all Big6 Skills in each context. For example, with one assignment, we might teach the Web and Task Definition; in a later unit we would emphasize Information Seeking Strategies or Evaluation. They key is to make the connection—to link students' learning about the Web into a relevant Big6 and curricular context.

When it comes to technology, we can't know it all or even anticipate what it might be. Remember the earlier quote from Bill Gates—in 20 years we will have computers that are a million times more powerful than those of today. No one really knows into what forms this capability will translate.

What we as educators can do is ask the key questions with the Big6 in mind:

- What do we want to accomplish—from a content and a Big6 perspective?

- How can the technology help to do it?

- In our schools, classrooms, libraries, labs, and homes—what will it take to use the technology in this way?

- Will this use really make a difference for students—in terms effectiveness and efficiency?

- Is it worth taking the time and effort to integrate the technology instruction now?

- If yes, what will it take? How can we provide meaningful learning opportunities that integrate content, process, and technology?

REFLECTIONS

REFLECTIONS

CHAPTER 4

Implementing The Big6: Context, Context, Context

Introduction: Contexts

In real estate, they talk about the three key elements: location, location, and location. We look at the key elements to implementing a meaningful Big6 information and technology skills program in a similar way: context, context, and context.

There are actually two essential contexts for successful Big6 Skills instruction: (1) the process itself and (2) real needs—either curricular or personal. When we talk about an integrated Big6 Skills program, we mean integrating Big6 learning and teaching in both of these contexts.

Another way to think of these contexts is as "anchors." When students are engaged in a task or solving a problem, it's easy to get lost. But, they are in a much better position to succeed if, at any point in time, they can identify the two anchors:

■ #1–Where are they in the Big6 process?

■ #2–What's the curriculum or personal need?

Let's look at each of these contexts in more detail.

Context 1: The Big6 Process

As explained in Chapter 2, the Big6 is a process composed of six stages of skills. While successful information problem-solving requires completion of all stages, the stages do not have to be completed in any particular order or in any set amount of time. A stage can be repeated or revisited a number of times. And, sometimes a stage is completed with little effort, while at other times a stage is difficult and time consuming.

Knowing where they are in the process is very helpful for students. It helps them to know what's been completed and what is still to do. When working on an assignment, project, report, or even an information problem of personal interest, students should be able to identify where they are in the process. For example, are they reading an article related to current events? That's Use of Information, Big6 #4. Are they searching for sources using a CD-ROM index? That's Big6 #3, Location & Access.

Similarly, teachers should frame instructional and learning experiences related to information and technology skills instruction within the Big6 process. Are they teaching *PowerPoint* for multimedia presentation? That's Synthesis, Big6 #5. Are students working with the library media specialist to determine possible sources for a project? That's Information Seeking Strategies, Big6 #2.

Anchoring instruction in individual skills within the overall Big6 process provides students with a familiar reference point. They see the connections among seemingly separate skills and are able to reflect on what came before and anticipate what comes after.

Therefore, we recommend continually working with students to help them recognize where they are in the process. Some ways that teachers can do this is by

- Identifying for students the various stages as they go through an assignment, project, or report

- Using a story or video to point out the Big6 stages related to the actions of one or more characters

- Modeling Big6 process recognition by pointing out when they themselves are engaging in a particular Big6 stage, and

- Asking students, verbally or in writing, to identify which Big6 stage they are working on.

Context 2: Curriculum

Information is a pervasive and essential part of our society and our lives. We are, at our essence, processors and users of information. This is not a recent development. Humans have always been dependent upon information to help them make decisions and guide their actions. The change has come in the sheer volume of information and the complexity of information systems—largely due to advances in information technology and the accelerated rate at which we live our lives.

Information is pervasive, and so are the Big6 information skills. Therefore, there are many opportunities for teaching and learning the Big6 Skills. From research and experience, we know that the Big6 Skills are best taught in the context of real needs—school or personal. Students today, more than ever, want to see connections between what they are learning and their lives. They want to know how something is relevant. This is no problem for the

That's why, in implementing Big6 instruction, we do not promote adding new curriculum content, units, or topics.

Big6, as the approach emphasizes applicability across environments and situations.

Most often in school settings, the context for Big6 Skills instruction is the actual classroom curriculum. This includes the subject area units and lessons of study, and most importantly, the assignments on which students will be evaluated. Throughout the school year, teachers and students engage in a rich range of curriculum subjects and topics. In fact, one of the current problems we face in education is "curriculum information overload"—there's just too much to cover in a limited time.

That's why, in implementing Big6 instruction, we do *not* promote adding new curriculum content, units, or topics. There's plenty going on in the curriculum already. The last thing that classroom teachers and students need is more content. Therefore, from a Big6 perspective, the challenge is to determine good opportunities for learning and teaching Big6 Skills within the existing curriculum. This involves the following:

1 Analyzing the curriculum to (a) select units and assignments that are well-suited to Big6 Skills instruction, and (b) determine which Big6 Skills are particularly relevant to the selected curriculum units and assignments

2 Developing a broad plan that links the Big6 to various curriculum units

3 Designing integrated unit and lesson plans to teach the Big6 in the context of the subject area curriculum.

We strongly advocate a collaborative approach to Big6 Skills instruction. That is, classroom teachers, library media specialists, technology teachers, and other educators can work together to analyze the curriculum, develop a broad plan, and design specific unit and lesson plans that integrate the Big6 and classroom content. These educators can also collaborate on teaching and assessment.

Analyzing Curriculum From a Big6 Perspective

As stated above, effective Big6 instruction starts with selecting existing curriculum units that are best suited to integrated Big6 Skills instruction. We refer to these units as "big juicies" —those information-rich curriculum units that are filled and dripping with Big6 potential. "Big juicy" units are rich in information needs, resources, and processing. These are the units that offer particularly good opportunities for teaching specific Big6 Skills within the overall Big6 process.

For example, we might select units that involve a report, project, or product rather than those that rely on a test for assessment. And, we probably wish to focus on units that require a range of multiple resources rather than the textbook. Desirable units should also involve a large number of students and span a reasonable time frame. Let's see how this might work in practice.

Third grade teacher, Ms. Hall, and library media specialist, Mr. Daley, review some of the units that Ms. Hall plans to teach during the school year. They agree there are three major units that result in some form of product or project, require lots of different types of resources, involve the whole class, and span more than just a week or two. These three units seem to be information-rich "big juicies."

> *We refer to these units as "big juicies" —those information-rich curriculum units that are filled and dripping with Big6 potential.*

- The planets unit: taught in the second quarter, taking one month, resulting in group presentations on each of the planets, and usually involving frequent trips to the library media center

- The endangered animals unit: taught at the end of the school year, taking four weeks, involves use of the WWW, resulting in individual *HyperStudio* productions and posters

- The unit on community: taught in October, taking six weeks, involving a series of worksheets that combine to make a short booklet.

What now? Do they select among these units or do they just integrate the Big6 with all three? Do they teach all the Big6 Skills with each unit or focus on specific Big6 Skills?

These choices must depend upon other factors including the time available for Big6 instruction and what else is going on during the school year. We do, however, recommend that while they review and reinforce the overall Big6 process with each unit, Ms. Hall and Mr. Daley should provide targeted Big6 Skills instruction on one or two of the specific skills. For example:

- The planets unit is a group project, so a lesson might be offered on defining tasks and dividing up the work (Big6 #1–Task Definition) and also on how to put it all together (Big6 #5–Synthesis). It might also be an opportunity to focus on Evaluation (Big6 #6) and provide instruction in assessing final products as well as their Big6 abilities.

- The endangered animals unit relies on both the *HyperStudio* and the WWW, so lessons could be taught on both. *HyperStudio* is a Synthesis tool, so that's a Big6 #5 lesson. Lessons on the Web could focus on Information Seeking Strategies (Big6 #2), Location & Access skills (Big6 #3), and recognizing and extracting relevant information—Use of Information (Big6 #4).

- The community unit comes earliest in the school year and lasts six weeks, the most time, so it is certainly a good choice for integrated instruction. Since it's early in the year, it might be a good unit in which to review the entire Big6 process. The various worksheets offer an opportunity for a specific lesson on Big6 #1–Task Definition. The frequent use of the library media center for resources is easily linked to lessons taught by the library media specialist on selecting from the range of resources available, Information Seeking Strategies (Big6 #2), and how to locate and access the resources and information within the resources, Location & Access (Big6 #3).

In practice, selecting units for integrated Big6 instruction and overall Big6 Skills planning really depends upon the specific needs of the students as well as the setting and situation. The ultimate goal is to provide frequent opportunities for students to learn and practice the Big6. Repetition is crucial. While these skills may seem to be simple or common sense at first, they actually are quite involved and can be difficult to master.

In terms of situation, Big6 planning and plans differ based on the setting and who is going to be involved, e.g., the classroom teacher, library media specialist, teaching team, technology teacher, entire grade level or subject area, school, or district. Examples of each of these situations are presented below.

Planning and Plans for the Individual Teacher

Classroom teachers organize and plan the school year around a series of curriculum units and lessons. Based on local or state curriculum guides, teachers determine the sequence of units, their general goals and objectives, and the time they will spend on each unit. While they frequently make adjustments during the school year, most teachers try to cover the intended units in sequence.

As described above, we suggest that teachers review their existing curriculum plans to determine opportunities to integrate Big6 Skills instruction. The task is to first identify units that have good potential for integrating Big6 Skills and then decide which Big6 Skills to emphasize with each unit.

Units that are good candidates for integrating Big6 Skills instruction generally:

- Are of longer duration
- Involve a report, project, or product rather than a quiz or test
- Use multiple resources
- Involve a range of teaching methods.

As noted, it is not necessary or desirable to teach all stages of the Big6 with each curriculum unit. The Big6 is applicable to any problem-solving situation, so students will have ample opportunity to work on the Big6 throughout the school year. Therefore, when students are first presented with an assignment as part of a curriculum unit, we recommend first "talking through" the assignment in the context of the overall Big6 process. Then, as students work through the assignment, the teacher, often in partnership with the library media specialist and technology teacher, can offer more in-depth lessons on one or more of the Big6 Skills. By the end of the school year, students in the class should have experienced a full range of Big6 lessons in the context of the real curriculum and the overall Big6 process.

Figure 4.1 is a sample "Big6 Skills by Unit Matrix" for Mr. Hancock, a 4th grade teacher. The Matrix is an efficient way to summarize integrated Big6 plans. (Note: the plans included here are composites of a number of teachers and settings. They do not actually refer to any specific school, district, or teacher.)

Figure 4.1 documents the units that Mr. Hancock intends to integrate with Big6 Skills instruction. Presented in the order they will be introduced in the school year (by Marking Period— M_Per), information is also included on the total time of instruction (noted in periods), the subject, assignments, and Big6 Skills slated for in-depth instruction. A large X indicates that a Big6 lesson will be taught while a small x indicates that the Big6 Skill will only be touched on. For example, the first unit is spelling, which is taught in a total of 40 periods over all four marking periods. The spelling unit is part of the language arts curriculum and is evaluated by a test. Mr. Hancock intends to teach a lesson on Big6 #4 – Use of Information—in conjunction with the spelling unit, focusing on strategies for learning and remembering correct spelling. Mr. Hancock will also mention Big6 #5– Synthesis—by reminding students how they are expected to present their answers on their spelling tests.

From Figure 4.1, we also see that Mr. Hancock uses the state history unit as a major kickoff to the Big6 process during the first and second marking periods. He will also spend a considerable amount of time over the entire year on Task Definition, Big6

> **The ultimate goal is to provide frequent opportunities for students to learn and practice the Big6. Repetition is crucial.**

#1. He does this with a range of assignments in nine different units including the following:

- Written report - state history
- Maps, product - geography
- Test - listening skills
- Oral report - deserts.

Mr. Hancock will also teach technology skills within the Big6 process and integrate the skills with specific curriculum units. Computer graphic software will be used to generate maps in the geography unit (which occurs twice during the school year); letter writing in the first marking period will use word processing software; and the interdisciplinary desert unit (in the 3rd marking period) will use full-text electronic resources and search the Web.

If developed at the beginning of the school year, the Big6 Skills by Unit Matrix becomes a blueprint for integrated information skills instruc-

Figure 4.1: Big6 Skills by Unit Matrix: Mr. Hancock—4th Grade Teacher

THE BIG6											
Unit	Subject	Assignment	M_Per	Pers	1	2	3	4	5	6	Comments
Spelling Arts	Language	Test	1234	40				X	–		strategies for learning/ remembering spelling
State History	Social	Written	12xx	30	X	X	X	X	X	X	major unit – lessons on all Big6
Geography	Social	Maps	1x3x	20	X			X			computer graphics to produce maps
Listening	Language Arts	Test	1xxx	10	X			X			note-taking, tape recording
Personal Hygiene	Health	Ads, Product	1xxx	15	X	–			–	X	evaluating ads, creating posters
Letter Writing	Language	Product	1xxx	15	X				X	X	what makes a good letter using word processing
Food	Health	Product (chart posters, ads)	x2xx	15	X	X	X	X			periodical indexes on CD and the web
Multiplication Tables-10	Math	Test	x2xx	20					–		just mention ways to memorize
Structure Plants	Science	Experiment Test	xx34	20					X		lab reports – can computer generate
Rocks and Minerals	Science	Worksheet Test	xx3x	20		X	X				use sources for worksheet – focus on brainstorm, narrow and keywords
Metric Measurements	Math	Test	xx3x	20		X	X				test will include examples of the metric system in action–will need sources
Deserts/Life Weather	Social Studies/ Science	Written and Oral Report	xx3x	30	X	X	X				2 subjects, lots of electronic information seeking strategies, location & access
Mixed Numbers	Math	Worksheet	xx3x	20						X	self-evaluation

tion. It can also be updated during the year to reflect what actually takes place. Therefore, at the end of the year, the Matrix offers detailed documentation of what was actually accomplished. The plans also serve as the basis for follow-up planning by the teacher for the next year *and* for other teachers who will have the same students the next year.

Planning and Plans for a Subject Area, Grade, or Team

While Big6 implementation through individual teachers is essential, it is also valuable to coordi-nate Big6 Skills instruction in broader contexts. This section explains how this can happen within a particular subject area, grade, or team.

Figures 4.2 and 4.3 offer two different matrix views of a 6th grade in a school. There are three teachers in this grade and each con-tributed four units. The data included are similar to figure 4.1; however, we have added a column for Teacher. Figure 4.2 is sorted by teacher and helps to see if all Big6 are covered in a curricu-lum context. Figure 4.3 shows the distribution of units across the year. It also helps to compare across teachers—to determine possible areas for collaboration and to help avoid conflicting demands for resources.

Figure 4.2: Big6 Skills by Unit Matrix: Grade 6   Sorted by Teacher

THE BIG6												
Unit	Subject	Teacher	Assignment	M_Per	Pers	1	2	3	4	5	6	Comments
Graphing	Math	CAE	Worksheets, Test	1xxx	20	X				X		*following instructions; using spreadsheet software*
Electricity	Science	CAE	Worksheets, Test	x2xx	15				X			*skimming and scanning*
Recycling	Social Studies/ Science	CAE	Oral Report with visuals	xx3x	20	X	X	X	X	X	X	*major activity; use Power Point; presentation*
Settling the West	Social Studies	CAE	Written Report, Test	xxx4	20	X			−	X	X	*difference between oral and written reports*
Map Skills	Social Studies	DJW	Maps, Product	1234	20	X				X	X	*year long; read and create reports*
Light	Science	DJW	Test, Lab	x2xx	20					X	X	*using textbook; word processing templates for labs*
Folktales and Legends	Language Arts	DJW	Product, Report	xx3x	30	X	X	X				*physical object, report, use of Web*
Poetry Tables-10	Language Arts	DJW	Short Written Assignment	xxx4	20				X	X	X	*reading poems, writing good poetry*
Currents Events	Social Studies	SEW	Short Reports	1234	40	X	X	X	X	X	X	*year long; write newspaper or TV stories; use WWW*
Vocabulary	Language Arts	SEW	Test	1xxx	5	X				X		*early in the year; understand directions; test-taking strategies*
Folktales and Legends	Language Arts	SEW	Homework, Test	x2xx	20				X		X	*comparing old and new*
Settling the West	Social Studies	SEW	Test, Report	xxx4	20		X	X		X		*key on writing*

For example, we see that over the entire school year, Ms. Eisner (CAE) provides emphasis on all of the Big6. She introduces Task Definition at the beginning of the year in conjunction with the math unit on graphs. She also integrates spreadsheet software into teaching students graphing concepts and how to create graphs. Skimming and scanning are important Use of Information skills and these are taught in the second marking period as part of the worksheet assignments on electricity. The major Big6 unit for Ms. Eisner is the recycling unit in the 3rd marking period. Here, the students complete an oral report using *PowerPoint*. And later, in the 4th marking period, the students learn the differences in presentation between oral and written reports.

Mr. Wilson (DJW) and Mrs. Walker (SEW) also have plans to integrate the Big6 and technology into their subject area units. Mr. Wilson does a nice job in spreading out various Big6 lessons. For example, he focuses on Use of Information and Synthesis in the first and second marking periods in both the map skills and light units. But then he works on Task Definition, Information Seeking Strategies, and Location & Access toward the end of the year in the poetry unit. Mrs. Walker uses the year-long current events unit to teach each of the Big6 over the course of the year. She expects significant improvement in

Figure 4.3: Big6 Skills by Unit Matrix: Grade 6   **Sorted by Marking Period**

THE BIG6											
Unit	Subject	Teacher	Assignment	M_Per	Pers	1	2	3	4	5	6	Comments
Current Events	Social Studies	SEW	Short Reports	1234	40	X	X	X	X	X	X	*year long; write newspaper or TV stories; use WWW*
Map Skills	Social Studies	DJW	Maps, Product	1234	20	X			X	X		*year long; read and create maps*
Graphing	Math	CAE	Worksheets, Test	1xxx	20	X				X		*following instructions; using spreadsheet software*
Vocabulary	Language Arts	SEW	Test	1xxx	5	X				X		*early in the year; understand directions; test-taking strategies*
Electricity	Science	CAE	Worksheets, Test	x2xx	15				X			*skimming and scanning*
Folktales and Legends	Language Arts	SEW	Homework, Test	x2xx	20				X		X	*comparing old and new*
Light	Science	DJW	Test, Lab	x2xx	20				X	X		*using textbook; word processing templates for labs*
Folktales and Legends	Language Arts	DJW	Product, Report	xx3x	30	X	X	X				*physical object, report, use of Web*
Recycling	Social Studies/ Science	CAE	Oral Report with Visuals	xx3x	20	X	X	X	X	X	X	*major activity; use PowerPoint presentation*
Poetry	Language Arts	DJW	Short Written Assignment	xxx4	20				X	X	X	*reading poems, writing good poetry*
Settling the West	Social Studies	CAE	Written Report, Test	xxx4	20	X			–	X	X	*difference between oral and written reports*
Settling the West	Social Studies	SEW	Report	xxx4	20		X	X		X		*key on writing*

students' information problem-solving abilities and academic performance by June.

Figure 4.3 is also useful for highlighting common units and time frames. Both Mr. Wilson and Ms. Walker teach Folktales and Legends but at different times and using different types of assignments. The matrix confirms that they should not compete for library media or technology resources and services; however, they may wish to discuss ways to collaborate in the future. Also, interestingly, Mrs. Walker is going to emphasize Big6 #4–Use of Information and Big6 #6–Evaluation in this unit. She plans on having students compare old and new folktales and use electronic resources through the library media center to do so. Mr. Wilson is focusing on the first three Big6 stages—Task Definition through Location & Access. He plans to have students use the Web to find information relevant to making some artifact and to make a report on it.

The plan also shows that Ms. Eisner's and Mrs. Wilson's students are working on a Settling the West unit at the same time. They may wish to coordinate efforts and share Big6 lessons. They also may wish to make sure there are adequate resources and services for both classes or make adjustments in the schedule.

Plans and Planning on the School Level

It is also important to plan for systematic Big6 Skills instruction at the school level. The goal is to ensure that students have a range of Big6 instructional experiences across grade levels and subjects. These experiences should build on each other so that by the end of their K–12 education, each student has had ample opportunities to develop competencies in specific technology and information skills within the overall Big6 context.

School-wide Big6 planning requires cooperation among classroom teachers, library media specialists, technology teachers, and administrators. From experience, we find that active, engaged library media specialists are in an ideal position to coordinate the school-wide Big6 Skills effort. First, information skills instruction is a major function of library media programs. In addition, library media specialists are involved with instruction across the curriculum. They are responsible for providing resources and services to all grades and subjects and gen-

Figure 4.4: Big6 Skills by Unit Matrix: Middle School   **Sorted by Grade Level and Marking Period**

THE BIG6												
GR	Tchr	Unit	Subject	Assignment	QTR	1	2	3	4	5	6	Comments
06–06	SEW	Current Events	SS	report	1234	X	X	X	X	X	X	*all year long - can hit all Big6*
06–06	ARB	Poetry	English	short written assignment	xxx4				X	X	X	*#4 – reading poems, #5/6 – writing good poetry*
07–07	SLJ	Graphs	Math	product	x2xx				X	X		*types of graphs and spreadsheet software*
07–07	TCH	Recycling	SS/Sci	product	x23x	–	X	X	–	X	–	*lots of technology*
08–08	HJW	Map Skills	SS	worksheet	1xxx		X		X			*use of maps*
08–08	TMJ	Noise	Sci	written report	x2xx	–	X	X		X	–	*build on grade 7, technology*
07–08	CER	Diet & Nutririon	Health	posters	1x3x	X	X	–	–	X	–	*health reaches all students; repeats 2x year*
07–08	CER	Tobacco & Smoking	Health	test	1x3x	X			X	X	X	*cooperative teacher, test-taking strategies & the Big6*

erally have an excellent overview of the existing school curriculum. Therefore, we recommend, when possible, that library media specialists coordinate Big6 planning with technology teachers, classroom teachers, administrators, and support staff.

Figure 4.4 is a partially completed Big6 by Unit Matrix for a middle school covering grades 6–8. At this point, the Matrix only includes some of the units slated for integrated Big6 instruction. The library media specialist is compiling this plan and has worked on documenting integrated units across the grade levels and subject areas. For example, she has locked two units in grades 6–8 and two additional units in the health curriculum that encompass students in grades 7 and 8. The health units are particularly useful since the teacher is very cooperative, the units involve a range of resources, and all students must take health at some point. The 6th grade current events unit is also an important one. Because it is carried out all year, there is a good opportunity to offer lessons in each of the Big6 Skills at some point in time.

While this middle school Matrix already shows a range of integrated skills instruction, there is considerable room for expansion. As the library media specialist contacts teachers, this plan will grow to document the full-school information and technology skills effort.

Summary

Systematic planning for integrated Big6 Skills instruction is essential if we are to make a difference in our classrooms and schools. If we truly believe that information and technology skills are essential for student success, then we must make sure that students have frequent opportunities to learn and practice these skills.

It's not enough to work with students one-on-one or to offer an isolated lesson in note-taking or Web search engines. Students need lessons in each of the Big6 Skills, delivered in the context of the real, subject area assignments. Accomplishing comprehensive, integrated Big6 instruction requires classroom teachers, library media specialists, technology teachers, and administrators to make a concerted and systematic effort to plan and document their efforts.

Figure 4.5: is a blank Big6 Skills by Unit Matrix to help get you started.

THE BIG6											
GR	Tchr	Unit	Subject	Assignment	QTR	1	2	3	4	5	6	Comments

REFLECTIONS

CHAPTER 5

Assesment of Information & Technology Skills

Introduction

While not always the most enjoyable part of learning and teaching, assessment is nevertheless essential to helping students attain higher levels of achievement. This is particularly important in relation to the Big6, as we believe that competence in information problem-solving is a key to success in every curriculum area.

By assessing students' skills in each of the Big6, we can pinpoint strengths and weaknesses and target areas for further development. We can also assess how well students are able to apply the Big6 process to a range of tasks and offer additional instruction as necessary.

Effective assessment should communicate teacher expectations, provide motivation, and enable students to assess themselves. To do so, educators should consider the following:

- The specific content-learning goals
- Related Big6 Skills
- Criteria for assessment, and
- Evidence to examine to determine student performance.

Assessment that focuses on instructional objectives and is based on established criteria helps teachers to appropriately modify and target instruction. Assessment can also help educators determine whether students are eligible for advanced instruction or if students need special, individualized assistance.

Assessment can be defined as making judgments based on a predetermined set of criteria. From a Big6 perspective, two broad criteria for assessment are effectiveness and efficiency.

Effectiveness and Efficiency

Two key criteria of assessment are part of stage #6–Evaluation—in the Big6 process:

- 6.1 Effectiveness of the product.
- 6.2 Efficiency of the process.

Students learn to assess the results of their efforts by analyzing the *effectiveness* of their product and their *efficient* use of the Big6 process to complete various tasks and create various products.

Even young children can learn to judge whether they are effective (having done a good job or worthy of a good grade) or efficient (not wasting time and effort). As students get older, they can assume more and more responsibility for their own achievement and assessment of that achievement.

In relation to effectiveness, students can learn to judge their own products. Students can diagnose the results of their effort when they learn to do such things as the following:

- Compare the requirements to the results
- Check the appropriateness and accuracy of the information they use
- Judge how well their solution is organized
- Rate the quality of their final product or performance compared to their potential (i.e., Did I do the best that I could?)
- Judge the quality of their product to a predefined standard.

These, of course, are rather sophisticated actions. But again, younger children can still ask themselves such questions as:

- Is my project good; how do I know?
- Am I proud of my project?

Assessing efficiency requires students to evaluate the nature, tendencies, and preferences of their personal information problem-solving process. This is sometimes referred to as "meta-cognition"—recognizing how we learn, process information, and solve problems. With the Big6, we can help students learn how to assess the efficiency of the process they use to reach decisions and solutions. Some techniques to facilitate this include the following:

- Keeping and evaluating a log of activities
- Reflecting back on the sequence of events and judging effort and time involved
- Reviewing and analyzing the areas of frustration and barriers they encountered
- Rating their abilities to perform specific information problem-solving actions. (i.e., locating, note-taking, skimming, scanning, prioritizing).

For younger children, efficiency-related questions include asking the following:

- Am I proud of my effort?
- What was easy and what was difficult?
- How could I do better next time?

These are the types of questions that teachers can build into activities and assignments.

This is sometimes referred to as "meta-cognition"— recognizing how we learn, process information, and solve problems.

Forms and Context for Assessment

There are actually two broad forms of assessment—summative and formative. Summative is after-the-fact assessment, designed to determine the degree of student learning after they have completed a lesson, unit, or other instructional event. Assessing students' performance on the overall information problem-solving process, through a project, report, or assignment for example, is summative assessment. Formative assessment involves providing feedback so that adjustments can be made before students turn in their work. Formative assessment of information and technology skills might involve assessing students' work at each stage of the Big6.

Classroom teachers, library media specialists and other educators can either provide feedback at each step of the information problem-solving process or when the assignment, project, or product is completed.

Throughout this book, we emphasize that the Big6 Skills are best learned in the context of real curriculum needs. School curriculum is rich and detailed at all grade levels, and Big6 Skills instruction can easily be integrated with a range of subjects and topics. Assessment of Big6 Skills is similarly best conducted within real curriculum contexts. That means finding ways to determine students' abilities in the overall process and individual Big6 Skills as they complete various homework assignments, projects, reports, products, and tests.

Most often, the focus of assessment is on evaluating how well students are doing with just the classroom content. Content learning is clearly of major importance. But, we must also be concerned with process skills as embodied by the Big6. How effective and efficient are students overall and in the specific skills necessary to solve information problems?

Effective assessment speaks to many audiences:

- To students—to let them know how they are doing and how they can improve
- To teachers—to help them determine whether students are learning the content and skills

- To parents—to keep them informed about their children's level of success and how they might help them.

Assessment should measure performance in a manner that is easily understood by all audiences. In addition, good assessment strategies

- Reflect the objectives of the lesson or unit
- Measure the behavior described by the objective
- Make certain that students fully understand all assessment criteria
- Provide constructive feedback on strengths and weaknesses.

Ways of Assessing

Assessing the Big6 Skills in context includes the following elements:

- Evidence to examine to determine student performance
- The specific content-learning goals
- Related Big6 Skills
- Criteria for judging
- A rating scale for judging, and
- The judgments themselves.

Evidence

As stated, assessment of Big6 Skills should take place within the context of real curriculum needs. In practice, that means looking carefully at assignments. For a given curriculum unit, teachers select one or more assignments to emphasize the importance of content and skills, to motivate students, and to evaluate student performance. In most instances, assignments will comprise the "evidence" of assessing Big6 learning. Other options include observing student performance, talking to students during or after working on an assignment, or having students engage in self-assessment activities. Typical assignments include the following:

- Homework
- Worksheets
- Exercises

- Reports or research papers
- Projects
- Quizzes or tests.

Content Learning Goals

Content learning goals include the skills and topics of the subject area curriculum. These can be established by individual classroom teachers or designated by a standard curriculum at the school, district, region, or state level.

Big6 Learning Goals

It is not necessary or desirable to assess all the Big6 in every assignment. In fact, it can become tedious to do so. Therefore, we encourage educators to focus assessment on the Big6 Skills that were (1) taught or (2) particularly important to the learning and assignment.

Criteria for Judging

Assessment criteria should be clearly defined statements of intended learner outcomes. Criteria should describe competence levels and should be designed to measure students' achievement toward instructional goals. For the Big6 Skills, criteria should relate to students' abilities in applying the Big6 to the content learning goals. To assist teachers, sample criteria statements for each stage of the Big6 are provided in Figure 5.1.

A Rating Scale for Judging

Rating scales are used as an indication of a student's learning state on criteria at a given point in time. The scale can be a simple numbered order, labels, or even symbols:

1 (low) to 5 (high)

Needs work	Okay	Well done	Super
Tadpole		Frog	

The younger the students, the more we suggest avoiding any numerical scales. The main point—teachers and students need to have a simple way to express their learning state.

Figure 5.1: Sample Criteria Statements for the Big6

Task Definition
The student demonstrates the ability to:
- Determine the information problem to be solved
- Clearly define the task
- Identify the important elements of the task
- Show complete understanding of the task and its parts
- Pick out key words embedded in a question
- Ask good questions
- Understand and follow printed and/or oral directions.

Information Seeking Strategies
The student demonstrates the ability to:
- Develop an approach to seeking a variety of materials
- Determine which information sources are most/least important
- Determine which information sources are most/least appropriate
- Demonstrate knowledge of relevant sources
- Recognize that information can be gained from many sources including investigation and observation
- Understand the value of human resources
- Use appropriate criteria for selecting sources, including readability, scope, authority, currency, usefulness, and format.

Location & Access
The student demonstrates the ability to:
- Gather resources independently
- Ask questions to obtain information
- Determine what sources are available
- Access appropriate information systems, including online databases, catalog—master list, and electronic multimedia.

Use of Information
The student demonstrates the ability to:
- Paraphrase the main idea accurately from written, visual, and/or oral source material
- Summarize the main idea from written, visual, and/or oral source material
- Distinguish facts from opinions
- Gather information carefully (read, listen, and/or view)
- Cite sources accurately.

Synthesis
The student demonstrates the ability to:
- Prepare an accurate bibliography of all resources (Internet and other resources)
- Organize information
- Present information
- Use a standard bibliographic format
- Prepare charts, graphs, outlines, etc.
- Compare and contrast points of view from several sources
- Summarize and retell information from multiple sources
- Design products to communicate content.

Evaluation
The student demonstrates the ability to:
- Assess projects for strengths and weaknesses
- Provide recommendations for improving the information problem-solving result
- Judge solutions and decisions
- Assess the completeness of the response to the assigned task
- Review and critique the steps used in solving an information problem.

The Judgments Themselves

In order to make developing and implementing judgments easier, we created Big6 Scoring Guides. These guides combine the various elements of assessment in a straightforward form. In the next section, we create Big6 Scoring Guides and give specific examples of a scoring guide in use.

Big6 Scoring Guides

In addition to pulling together all the requisite elements of assessment, Big6 Scoring Guides are designed to communicate teachers' expectations for students' work in ways that students can understand and use. Big6 Scoring Guides focus on the information problem-solving process as well as the final result. Therefore, guides are useful both during and after working on assignments—for both formative and summative assessment.

As stated above, formative assessment involves diagnosing students' performance during learning so that adjustments can be made before students turn in their work. Adjustments may include the following:

■ Redirecting planned instruction to focus on areas where students are having trouble

■ Providing special learning activities not previously planned

■ Helping students to apply relevant technology tools

■ Redefining the problem or returning to a previous Big6 stage

■ Offering one-on-one tutoring

■ Brainstorming alternative approaches.

These types of adjustments are prescriptions for improving learning. Of course, Big6 Scoring Guides can also be used to assess final products—summative assessment. Many teachers find that post-assignment debriefings —built around Big6 Scoring Guides—are effective ways to involve students in the assessment process.

It's relatively easy to create a Big6 Scoring Guide:

1. Define the curriculum objectives within a Big6 context.

2. Determine which Big6 Skills are important (the focus) for the particular assignment.

3. Develop criteria across a scale (i.e., from "highly competent" to "not yet acceptable"). There may be more than one aspect to each criterion. Consider which aspects are essential.

4. Determine what evidence will be examined to determine student performance for each Big6 Skill.

5. Conduct the assessment.

6. Share the assessment with students.

7. Determine and document the level of achievement.

8. Revise as necessary.

Figure 5.2 is an elementary curriculum example that uses a Big6 Scoring Guide in context. The companion Scoring Guide is Figure 5.3. The curriculum context is a science lab experiment on the effects of light on seed growth. The Scoring Guide shows that only three Big6 Skills are being assessed: Location & Access, Use of Information, and Synthesis. The level of student performance for each skill is indicated from high to low—scientist to student. Teachers can use the Big6 Scoring Guide to assess students on different aspects of the Big6 within the context of the assignment. The Scoring Guide can also be used to help students assess themselves. We are strong proponents of student self-assessment as explained in the next section.

Self-Assessment

Continuous self-assessment is an integral part of the Big6. When students engage in Big6 #6–Evaluation—activities, they are conducting self-assessment. In addition to having students reflect on their own abilities, self-assessment

Elementary Science Laboratory Experiment: Light and Seed Growth

Objectives:

1. To study the impact of light on seed growth.

2. To gather necessary materials and conduct an experiment.

3. To keep a daily journal of observations.

4. To write up a lab and draw logical conclusions.

Procedures:

Working in pairs, students are to:

1. Line two glasses with paper towels and stuff the inside of the glasses with more paper towels to hold the paper towel liner against the glass.

2. Place four bean seeds, evenly spaced and halfway down, between the glass and the paper towels.

3. Dampen the paper towels with water.

4. Put one glass in a dark cupboard or cabinet and place the other glass on a windowsill.

5. Each day, keep the paper towels in each glass moist.

6. Make observations in a journal each day for seven days. Note date, time, actions taken, and observations.

7. Write up the experiment in scientific lab format. Include a written summary of results and a conclusion based on observations.

© 1999 Eisenberg & Berkowitz. Published by Linworth Publishing, Inc.

fosters independence and responsibility in students. Through self-assessment, students learn to translate expectations into action, build on their accomplishments, and work on weaknesses.

Teachers can reinforce self-assessment by involving students in developing criteria, grading schemes, and Big6 Scoring Guides. Teachers can also help students to generalize from "school-work assessment" (e.g. on projects, tests,

assignments) to success in areas of personal interest (e.g. sports, art, music, hobbies) and ultimately at work (e.g. job satisfaction, salary, making a contribution).

It is difficult, if not impossible, for students to do their best if they don't know how to recognize it when they see it. All too often, students are left to guess at such things as whether they are finished with an assignment or whether they have done a good job on an assignment. Students should be able to compare their efforts with their teachers' expectations and with established standards. When necessary, students need to revise or redirect their effort. And, self-assessment may result in students realizing that they need to learn new skills.

We believe it is crucial to help students learn to do the following:

- Assess their own information problem-solving styles

- Value and recognize quality work

- Reflect on the ways they go about tackling assignments and tasks

- Determine how they can improve, and

- Learn how to establish criteria to evaluate their results.

Students don't often take the initiative to self-assess because they haven't been encouraged to do so, may not see the value in self-assessment, or may not know how to do so. That's where the Big6 approach comes in. The Big6 reminds us that evaluation is essential to the process. Teachers must prepare students to learn self-assessment in the context of curriculum, personal, or work situations.

Feelings are an important part of self-assessment. Students may lack confidence and pride in their work because they don't really know if they have done a good job. Sometimes feelings of confidence and pride are replaced with frustration and disappointment when students get their assignment back with a poor grade when they expected to do well. Self-assessment helps students and teachers apply the same evaluation criteria to the students' work.

Figure 5.3: Big6 Scoring Guide for Elementary Science Laboratory Experiment

	Expert Scientist	Scientist	Lab Assistant	Student
Location & Access	Gathers lab materials: independently appropriately	Gathers lab materials: with some assistance appropriately	Needs assistance: missing some materials	Needs assistance: missing most materials
Use of Information	Journal includes: daily entries; appropriate to task; accurate	Journal includes: almost daily entries; appropriate to task; accurate	Journal includes: some entries; inappropriate to task; accurate or inaccurate	Journal includes: few or no entries
Synthesis	Lab write-ups complete and has proper format. Logical conclusion based on results.	Lab write-up not complete or problems with format. Logical conclusion based on results.	Lab write-up okay. Conclusion needs work.	Problems with lab write up and/or format. Conclusion needs work.

© 1987 Eisenberg & Berkowitz. Published by Linworth Publishing, Inc.

Students learn to look at their work through their teachers' eyes. In this way, students can build on strengths and identify areas for improvement. Students gain insight into specific areas to improve their performance. This can boost confidence, pride, and a higher level of academic success.

We often assume that students are able to rate the quality of their products or the effectiveness of their information problem-solving approach, but of course, this is not always the case. Self-assessment skills should not be assumed—they should be part of the instructional program. Students need to learn, recognize, and apply the standards of excellence. Again, it's helping students to learn to view their own work in the way teachers view students' work.

Summary

Assessment is an important part of learning and essential to learning the Big6 Skills. As with Big6 Skills instruction, Big6 assessment should be integrated with classroom curriculum. Existing assignments provide ample opportunities to assess individual Big6 Skills as well as overall information problem-solving

abilities. There are requisite elements to assessment, which are pulled together in the Big6 Scoring Guides. We include a blank scoring guide (Figure 5.4) to help you get started.

This blank guide is designed to include multiple assessments—by student (S), teacher (T), or library media specialist (L). This allows students and teachers to quickly identify gaps in their views of perceived performance. Focusing on gaps can lead to clarification of misunderstandings and highlight the need for further instruction.

The column labeled "Evidence" is used to indicate the products or techniques to use to assess specific skills. Examples of evidence include written, visual, or oral products, assignments, homework, projects, tests, observation, or even self-reflection. This is an essential piece of the Scoring Guide since it identifies the specific context for assessing student performance.

The last column, "Focus," relates to the relative importance of each skill being evaluated. It is not necessary or desirable to assess all Big6 Skills equally in every learning situation. The assigned focus should be based on the goals and objectives of the unit in terms of Big6 Skill development and content learning.

Figure 5.4: Blank Big6 Scoring Guide

Big6™ Assessment Scoring Guide									
Criteria									
Big6™ Skills		Highly Competent		Competent		Adequate		Not Yet Acceptable	Evidence	Focus
Eisenberg/ Berkowitz © 1997		10 points		8 points		7 points		5 points		
1. Task Definition	S		S		S		S			
1.1 Define the problem.										
1.2 Identify the information needed.	T		T		T		T			
	L		L		L		L			
2. Information Seeking Strategies	S		S		S		S			
2.1 Determine all possible sources.	T		T		T		T			
2.2 Select the best sources.										
	L		L		L		L			
3. Location & Access	S		S		S		S			
3.1 Locate sources.										
3.2 Find information within sources.	T		T		T		T			
	L		L		L		L			
4. Use of Information	S		S		S		S			
4.1 Engage (e.g., read hear, view, and touch).										
4.2 Extract relevant information.	T		T		T		T			
	L		L		L		L			
5. Synthesis	S		S		S		S			
5.1 Organize information from multiple sources.	T		T		T		T			
5.2 Present the result.										
	L		L		L		L			
6. Evaluation	S		S		S		S			
6.1 Judge the result.										
6.2 Judge the process.										
	T		T		T		T			
	L		L		L		L			

S-Student, T-Teacher, L-Library Media Specialist

REFLECTIONS

REFLECTIONS

The **BIG6**

Teaching Technology & Information Skills

PART 2

The Big6 in Action

The first section of this book sets out the theoretical framework of the Big6 and in general terms describes how it is applied in various contexts. However, general terms are insufficient to fully appreciate how the Big6 operates.

Part II of this book presents the Big6 in action through further explanations, sample integrated lesson plans, and Big6 activities. We will take you through each Big6 component. We will guide you with Teaching Information Problem-solving ("TIPS") explanations applicable to each Big6 Skill and answer commonly asked questions. Perhaps the most valuable features of this section are the sample lesson plans. They encompass a variety of grades and subject matter. As part of an integrated curriculum, they demonstrate how the various aspects of the Big6 can be taught together or as separate skills. These lessons are for demonstration purposes only. You will want to extract ideas from them, explore other approaches and possibilities, and adapt the content to your program's needs. We cannot overemphasize these points—the sample lessons and activities should be adapted to your local situation and needs.

We encourage you to use this section of the book as an "idea generator." As you work to develop your students' information problem-solving skills, the first section will provide you with direction concerning why you do what you do. The second section will help you think of effective ways to do what you do. Think of it as a Big6 challenge for you personally. That is, approach each lesson's goals and objectives as your own information problem to solve. In designing your instructional units and lessons you need to define the task, identify a range of sources that will help you create an appropriate lesson, find the right set of sources, use the information within the sources, actually create the lesson, and evaluate whether your students actually learned the skills you intended your lesson to teach.

So use the Big6 as your guide to developing curriculum and instruction. After all, as educators we are best able to teach those skills we mastered by practice and implementation ourselves.

CHAPTER 6

The BIG 6

Big6™ Tips: Task Definition

Task Definition is the first stage in the Big6 process. Task Definition has two components:

1.1 Define the problem.
1.2 Identify the information needed.

Task Definition is a key to success in homework, assignments, and tests, yet it is often ignored or overlooked in terms of specific, formal instruction. Teachers don't intentionally give vague or confusing assignments, but students often have trouble understanding what's expected of them. In our *Helping With Homework* book, we describe a situation where I spoke to a class about a test they were supposed to have on the following Monday. Only about one-quarter of the class really knew what was going to be on the test, the type of test they would be taking, and what material they should study. Yes, the teacher had gone over the directions, but the students hadn't really "heard" it. Perhaps they were daydreaming, had something else on their minds, or truly didn't understand the directions.

The solution to this problem is not for the teacher to go over the assignment again, but to help the students assume responsibility for their own tasks. We want to move the focus of responsibility for the assignment from the teacher to the students. For example, we encourage students to do "brain surgery" on their teachers. "Get inside your teachers' heads—quiz the teachers on expectations, criteria for assessment, and key elements. Don't let the teacher move on to something else until you fully understand all aspects of the assignment."

One tip to encourage student responsibility is to purposely give assignments without much explanation. "You are to create travel brochures on countries." That's all the direction you need to give. This method forces the students to find out the details and can lead to a stimulating exchange on options, key aspects, and grading.

Another goal for Task Definition instruction is transferability—to have students apply their skills and knowledge beyond school situations. A hallmark of the Big6 is its broad applicability. While most library skills instruction centers on reports or projects, we encourage working on Task Definition with a wide range of tasks and problems.

All students have curriculum-based information problems to solve, for example:

- A kindergarten group learning about signs of spring
- A 3rd grade class making charts on food groups
- 6th graders studying why certain animal species are endangered
- 12th grade language arts students studying modern world authors
- A university economics class analyzing the impact of the Internet on global markets.

But we need to help students recognize that the Big6 also applies to problems and tasks they face every day, for example:

- Deciding what television show to watch
- Preparing for a basketball game
- Picking out a birthday present for a friend.

So, in addition to applying the Big6 to specific curriculum situations, teachers and library media specialists can work together to develop lessons that develop skills related to everyday situations. Lessons built around these and other personal information tasks have proved extremely motivating and useful in helping students recognize how the Big6 can be applied to lots of different situations.

For example, we like to organize students in triads—where students assume one of three roles—a talker who explains a problem, a listener/questioner who probes for detail, and a recorder who writes it all down. Later the students switch roles so that each one has a chance to do all three. Finally, the students report back on the problem they recorded (not on their own)—orally to the whole class, in writing to the teacher, or both.

Another tip is to have students keep a "Task Definition Log" for a week or so. Work with the students to develop (1) the criteria for what makes a task or problem, (2) what data they will record, and (3) a chart for recording the data. The logs can be discussed each day as well as summarized in final presentations that delve into the nature of tasks and problems, and how information, the Big6 Skills, and technology relate to them.

All of the above tips focus on the "defining the problem" component of Task Definition. In the Big6 model, Task Definition also includes "identifying the information" requirements of the problem. Here, we want students to consider various aspects of the information they will need to solve the task/problem—before they begin thinking about specific resources. For example, we want students to reflect on things like:

- The type of information (facts, opinions; primary or secondary)
- The amount of information (single source, a few resources, comprehensive)
- The format of information (text, graphics, audio, video).

These considerations are especially important today since technology is providing many different options for packaging information. Tips to help students learn to focus on information requirements include lessons where they brainstorm options related to their curriculum tasks and assignments. We've also found it useful to develop a checklist where students can indicate the types, amounts, and formats of information they are seeking.

With a solid idea of their information requirements, students are ready to move on and determine and select possible resources—Big6 #2.

The Big6™ Skills Approach to Information Problem-Solving

1. Task Definition
1.1 Define the problem
1.2 Identify the information needed

2. Information Seeking Strategies
2.1 Determine all possible sources
2.2 Select the best sources

3. Location & Access
3.1 Locate sources
3.2 Find information within sources

4. Use of Information
4.1 Engage (e.g., read, hear, view)
4.2 Extract relevant information

5. Synthesis
5.1 Organize info from multiple sources
5.2 Present the result

6. Evaluation
6.1 Judge the result (effectiveness)
6.2 Judge the process (efficiency)

©Eisenberg and Berkowitz, 1987

Title: Common Questions

Author: Barbara A. Jansen

Related Big6 Skills: Big6 #1–Task Definition

Purpose: The purpose of this exercise is to help students generate a list of questions that the class will use when locating information.

Learning Contexts: This strategy is applicable across subject areas (grades 4–6) where teachers want students to locate the same information about varied topics.

Discussion: This lesson provides a strategy for Task Definition. Students make a list of common questions for Big6 #1.2 (Identify the information needed). Many times, students need to find out the same information about different topics within a unit. For example, a third grade class may be studying biographies about notable Americans. The teacher knows that while each student or group of students is studying about a different person, they will need basically the same information. Instead of the teacher telling the students the information to find, students can participate in an activity to generate the list of questions (with the teacher's final approval, of course). This strategy gives students the responsibility for determining what information is important to know. The teacher can help with wording questions appropriately and has the option to add more questions if needed.

Sample in Context: Students in groups will brainstorm a list of questions that they need to find out about their topic. For example, a fifth grade class is studying the world's explorers. One group brainstorms a list of questions about Christopher Columbus and another group lists questions about Vasco de Gama. Once all groups are finished and their questions are hanging on large chart paper for all to see, have the groups walk around to read each list of questions, finding questions that are similar in content to their own. The teacher can place the charts around the room and set a timer for groups to rotate from chart to chart. Then have a class discussion on which questions are similar on each chart. The teacher will write common questions on the overhead, rewording them as needed (since groups may use various wording to mean the same thing), and make a list of several questions that all students will use for Big6 #1.2. The teacher can add questions that she knows will be important to the list. Students may also find information that may be unique to their topic.

Title: It's a Problem! Turning Curriculum Objectives into Problems for Students to Solve

Author: *Barbara A. Jansen*

Related Big6 Skills: *Big6 #1–Task Definition*

Purpose: *The purpose of this lesson is to motivate students to engage in the Big6 process and content study.*

Learning Contexts: This lesson is applicable across all subject areas in elementary settings where teachers want to provide a context for engaging in the curriculum content.

Discussion: In this lesson, teachers introduce an information problem and students determine solutions to the information problem. In the book *Information Problem-Solving: The Big Six Approach to Library and Information Skills*, (1990) the Big6 is presented in three levels, general to specific: Level I (individual's need for a process to solve information problems); Level II (The Big6 six-step process); and Level III (the twelve sub-skills).

Level I states that "whenever students are faced with an information problem (or with making a decision that is based on information), they can use a systematic, problem-solving process"(p. 21). Of course the approach is the Big6! More often than not, however, Level I of the Big6 is not addressed, and teachers state the task for the students by giving them the assignment. Therefore, the students do not have to engage in the first step of the Big6 process, nor do they have a reason to do so. Teachers and librarians can provide a need for students to use the Big6 as that "systematic approach" by presenting curriculum objectives as problems for students to solve and letting the students define the task. This will help students become aware that a process is required to solve problems in which information is needed to produce a solution.

Sample in Context: Instead of telling students that they will be opening their textbooks to Chapter 12 to study a particular unit or objective, create an information problem that will motivate them to want to learn the content and engage in the Big6 process in order to accomplish it. Once the information problem is presented, the teacher or librarian will guide students through a brainstorming session to define a task. (See "What's the Task?" p. 61.)

Examples: Fourth grade instructional objectives as prescribed by the State of Texas: (A) explain the meaning of selected patriotic symbols and landmarks, including the six flags over Texas, San Jose Mission, and the San Jacinto Monument; (B) sing or recite "Texas, Our Texas"; (C) recite and explain the meaning of the pledge to the Texas flag; and (D) describe the origins and significance of state celebrations such as Texas Independence Day and Juneteenth.

Information problem presented to students: "Students new to our school do not understand Texas symbols and state holidays. What can we do?" The teacher or librarian will further explain the information problem and then guide the students through a brainstorming session to define the task.

- First grade instructional objective: Create and use simple maps to identify the location of places in the classroom, school, community, and beyond.

  Information problem presented to students: "Your friend needs the directions to your house from school so that her mom can bring her to play with you after school. What can you do?" The teacher or librarian will further explain the information problem and then guide the students through a brainstorming session to define the task.

- Second grade instructional objective: (A) Identify characteristics of living organisms, and (B) identify characteristics of non-living objects.

  Information problem presented to students: "Students in kindergarten are studying the differences in living and nonliving objects. What can we do to help them understand this concept?" When students need to teach a skill or concept to others, they are more likely to learn it better themselves. This "problem" works well with many objectives in upper grades, requiring older students to teach to younger ones.

- Third grade instructional objective: Identify and explain simple machines.

  Information problem presented to students: "You are the superintendent on a construction site. The newest worker is from another country and doesn't know the names of simple tools or doesn't understand how they work. What is your task?"

- Fourth grade instructional objective: Describe the physical characteristics and indigenous animals of the desert biome.

  Informational problem presented to students: "Your car has broken down in the desert. You need to know about the biome in order to survive. What is your task?"

Title: What Information Do I Need to Do This Task?

Author: *Barbara A. Jansen*

Related Big6 Skills: *Big6 #1–Task Definition*

Purpose: *The purpose of this lesson is to help students identify information needed to do the task: Big6 #1.2–Identify the information need.*

Learning Contexts: This lesson is applicable across subject areas in elementary school settings (grades 3–6) where teachers and librarians want students to begin learning how to narrow the topic and identify information needed to do the task.

Discussion: In this lesson, students identify information needed to accomplish the task. Too often, teachers and librarians not only define the task for the students, but also tell students exactly the information that they need to find. Instead of doing the thinking for them, educators should provide opportunities for students to identify needed information. If young students put the task in the form of a question, then they will know to find "answers" to the questions. Students will construct many of the required questions as well as some questions not considered by the teacher and librarian. This gives students an ownership for the information they will locate and motivates them to engage in the information search since these are questions of interest to them. Teachers and librarians can still give students specific questions that are prescribed by the curriculum; however, they will do this after students have had the opportunity to devise the questions themselves.

Sample in Context: Students are placed in groups to construct the questions they need to answer in order to do the defined task. One student will record so the group members may focus on the thought process and not on the recording process. The teacher and librarian will circulate among the groups to give advice and assist as needed. When groups have completed their list of questions, the teacher and librarian will overhead project prepared questions that students will add to their list if not already included. This way, educators can prescribe the information needed, but students have the opportunity to create their own questions first.

Have students identify reoccurring topics or themes and categorize the questions.

Students will use highlighters to color-code each question according to topic or theme.

Write the topical questions on data charts (one topic per chart is a good way to organize) for note-taking during Big6 #4.

Title: What's the Task?

Author: *Barbara A. Jansen*

Related Big6 Skills: *Big6 #1–Task Definition*

Purpose: *The purpose of this exercise is to provide students with opportunities to define the task.*

Learning Contexts: This lesson is applicable across subject areas in elementary settings where teachers and librarians are trying to educate independent learners.

Discussion: In this exercise, students practice defining tasks and identifying the information they need to complete their tasks. The aim is to have students assume more responsibility in deciding what it really takes to complete an assignment. Teachers often assume too much ownership of an assignment by listing and defining all the specifics and details. In these situations, teachers are really doing the work of defining the task. Here, we try to turn it around. The students are given a broad assignment and asked to determine what it will take to complete the assignment successfully. The lesson also helps students to make the link between task and information by asking about the types and amount of information needed to solve the task as defined.

Sample in Context: The teacher explains an assignment in general terms verbally and with a handout. The teacher or library media specialist then asks the students to look at the assignment from a Big6 viewpoint. (If the students are unfamiliar with the Big6, this is the time to offer a short overview. If the students already know the Big6, provide a two-minute quick review.)

Taking a Big6 view means first focusing on Task Definition and asking, "What is the task?" and "What are all the things you need to do to solve the problem?" Break the class into groups of three or four. They should brainstorm what must be done in order to complete the assignment. One student in the group will record the ideas. Allow five to fifteen minutes for groups to generate a list of the details and specifics of the assignment. Then, ask the students to consider the information needed for the assignment: how much information, what formats would be best, etc. When time is up, record each group's list on the overhead projector or use a large screen display and word processor.

The teacher or librarian will reflect and ask key questions as the groups present, such as:

■ "It looks like what you mean by these suggestions is that we need to learn about _____ in order to solve the problem."

■ "Are you sure you will have enough variety of information?"

■ "You all seem to have a good sense of the various parts of the problem. How do you plan to present the results? What are your alternatives?"

Again, we are trying to get the students to focus on the problem, assume ownership, and consider the range of options available to them.

REFLECTIONS

CHAPTER 7

Big6™ Tips:
Information Strategies—
"Determine and Narrow"

This TIPS focuses on the second stage in the Big6 process—**Information Seeking Strategies**—which has two components:

2.1 Determine all possible sources.
2.2 Select the best sources.

Once students understand their task and the information requirements of the problem (stage #1–Task Definition), their attention should turn to the information sources to meet the task. Teachers, students, and even teacher-librarians sometimes talk about "seeking or finding the information needed" as one action. However, in the Big6 approach we break this down into two stages—first determining the most appropriate information sources for the situation (Information Seeking Strategies) and then finding the sources and the information in the sources (Location & Access).

Working with students to hone their Information Seeking Strategies can be mind-expanding and fun. We recommended a simple but powerful technique—**determine and narrow**.

"Determine and narrow" is used throughout the Big6 approach (for example, in Task Definition to select a topic or in Synthesis to determine an effective presentation format). "Determine and narrow" is also the essential process for Information Seeking Strategies. Here, we want students to open their minds and brainstorm all possible information sources to meet the task, and then critically determine the best sources for completing this particular task at this time.

When starting a report or paper, students typically turn to the standard sources—books, reference materials, or magazines. These may be highly appropriate, but students should also consider databases, electronic resources, community resources, experts, World Wide Web sites, businesses, various non-profit agencies, video- or audiotapes, and more. In our personal lives, we generally turn to other people for information (for example, for advice on buying a product or directions on how to get somewhere). But in school situations, we tend to look at printed or electronic sources. Our goal is to have students think broadly, to consider the full range of sources, and then select the most relevant sources for a particular task.

In developing Information Seeking Strategy skills, we first try to get students thinking as "far-out" as possible. For example, students working on assignments related to volcanoes and earthquakes might first think about encyclopedias or books on volcanoes. These are fine, but we also want them to recognize "visiting Mt. St. Helens" or "talking to a volcano expert" as possible sources. And, while in the past these might have been impractical to implement, actually locating and accessing these sources is possible today through the Internet. For example, you can visit Mt. St. Helens, The U.S. Geological Survey Website at *http://vulcan. wr.usgs.gov/Volcanoes/MSH/* or Volcano World's "Ask a Volcanologist" through *http://volcano.und.nodak.edu/vwdocs /ask_a.html.*

With more information sources available than ever before, the "narrowing" part of Information Seeking Strategies is more important than ever. Students need to learn that while there may be a number of sources to meet their needs, they must select sources carefully depending upon their situation and personal skill level. For example, a carefully written and easy-to-use encyclopedia rather than the U.S. Geological Survey Web site may better serve elementary students who know little about volcanoes. This site would be more suitable for high school seniors, while the "Volcano World" Web site is probably too general and simple for a high school senior's needs.

Rather than giving students the criteria for making selections, have them identify the criteria

Students need to learn that while there may be a number of sources to meet their needs, they must select sources carefully depending upon their situation and personal skill level.

for determining relevant sources. You'll be pleasantly surprised when they develop a list similar to the following:

- Accuracy
- Completeness
- Reliability (is authoritative)
- Preciseness
- Validity (is on target)
- Availability
- Currency
- Ease-of-use
- Cost
- Entertainment (is fun).

Which of these criteria are most important? It all depends on the situation and the student. Is the student working on a short written assignment or a senior thesis? Is the due date next week, next month, or tomorrow? Is the student just learning to read or a highly skilled information processor?

One of the most valuable things for students to learn is that for a short homework assignment it may be fine to use readily available and easy-to-use sources such as their textbook, a slightly dated encyclopedia, or even someone's personal Web site. However, for a major report or term project they would need to use more authoritative, accurate, and complete sources such as current books, authoritative journal articles, and the Web.

Title: It's an Armadillo

Author: *Tami J. Little (original lesson by Amy Eaton)*
Related Big6 Skills: *Big6 #2–Information Seeking Strategies, Big6 #4 –Information Use*
Purpose: *The students will learn to use a KWL (**K**now, **W**ant to know, and **L**earned) chart as well as a Fact-Finding Sheet.*

Learning Contexts: This lesson is applicable across content areas and grade levels.

Discussion: As a class, students use a KWL chart (see KWL Chart sample) to discover what they **Know**, what they **Want** to know, and what they have **Learned**. After completing the KWL chart, students will complete the Armadillo Fact Sheet as required by the teacher. The students read a non-fiction article in their basal reader about armadillos. The teacher decided to extend the learning to help the students discover more information about armadillos.

The students have had some experience with a KWL chart from previous grades. In the second grade, the students go to the library to work with the librarian to complete a KWL chart. The librarian works with the students to discuss what they all ready Know about the armadillo. Then, the librarian guides the students to ask questions about what they Want to know about the armadillo.

Next, the students access the Internet and complete the Armadillo Fact Sheet (see Fact Sheet sample). The teacher bookmarks the Web sites about the armadillo. Teachers assist students in accessing the sites and locating the information. Students will complete the fact sheet to the best of their abilities.

Finally, the teacher brings closure to the lesson by asking the students what they have Learned about the armadillo.

Sample in Context: We discovered from teaching this lesson that the students really do not need to access many Web sites. For some students, just viewing the pictures of the armadillos was an exciting task. The students who had difficulty reading needed assistance in order to successfully complete this lesson.

For follow-up, students drew a picture of an armadillo. Curriculum connections may include distinguishing fact and fiction by students writing stories such as, "My Friend the Armadillo." Students can access other animals or view animals on the online zoos.

The students have a story in their basal reader by Marc Brown about Arthur the aardvark. Students can compare and contrast Arthur the aardvark to the armadillo by telling what is the same and different. Students use the letter A as a starter for doing some creative story writing about animals with each letter of the alphabet as the beginning. (Example: A armadillo, B bear, C cow.)

The teacher and the librarian collaborated to write a letter home to parents, describing the lesson and giving them the Web sites to access from home or the public library (see sample letter). Parents were excited to see the fact sheet and the pictures their children drew of the armadillo and to read the letter telling them about the lesson.

K-W-L Chart on Armadillos

What I __Know__ about Armadillos.	What I __Want__ to know about Armadillos.	What I __Learned__ about Armadillos.

Armadillo Fact Sheet

Access the Web sites in order to answer the questions below. Use the bookmarks on your computer or type the address in the location bar.

http://www.kiva.net/~drdillo/dillogif.htm
http://www.tpwd.state.tx.us/nature/wild/mammals/dillo.htm

Name one type of armadillo.

Tell two things about the armadillo.

Write one thing about armadillos and their babies.

Write an interesting fact about an armadillo.

Print one picture of an armadillo.

Dear Parents,

The second grade students read a non-fiction article in their textbook about armadillos. This encouraged students to learn more about the armadillo. Students worked with Mrs. Little in the library to complete a **KWL chart** to help them identify what they **K**now, **W**ant to know, and **L**earned about armadillos. Notice the K, W, and L stand for the first letters of the action they were doing!

Students accessed the encyclopedia and non-fiction books as well as Internet Web sites. Remember that any time students want to access the Internet at home, they should do so with permission from you, the parents. It is important to set rules and guidelines with your child so that they know what is expected of them when they are using the Internet. If you do not have Internet access at home, check for access at the public library.

Here is a list of the Web sites the students used to locate information:

http://www.kiva.net/~drdillo/dillogif.htm
http://www.tpwd.state.tx.us/nature/wild/mammals/dillo.htm

If you want to do some searching on the Internet, try Yahooligans, a search engine just for children. The address is *http://www.yahooligans.com/*

Sincerely,

Your child's teacher

Title: What Can I Use for This Project? Teaching Students to Select Resources

Author: *Barbara A. Jansen*

Related Big6 Skills: *Big6 #2–Information Seeking Strategies*

Purpose: *The purpose of this lesson is to teach students to select appropriate resources.*

Learning Contexts: This lesson is applicable across subjects with students (grades 3–8) who are having problems distinguishing appropriate resources.

Discussion: Young students (grades 3–8) need considerable guidance in identifying appropriate resources for specific tasks. If research is presented within the framework of an information problem-solving model, then the process of selecting resources is naturally included. With the plethora of reference titles (electronic and traditional print) available today, along with the primary sources of observation and subject experts, we cannot possibly expect students to know numerous specific titles. Students in grades 3–8 can begin to learn general types of resources such as general and subject encyclopedias, atlases, almanacs, books, and the availability of human experts. For each assignment, educators need to introduce the specific resources that the students can use, but may not yet be able to identify on their own.

Item: Students learn the process of exclusion by developing a list of potential resources and selecting the best sources from that range of resources.

Sample in Context: Determining and narrowing and "The Process of Exclusion." Once the task has been defined, students need to determine the range of possible resources available for completing the task. Essential skills for information problem-solving process include brainstorming all possible sources and narrowing the list to the best ones (Eisenberg & Berkowitz, 1990, p. 6). One strategy, called "Process of Exclusion," has the students brainstorm a list:

1. Each group of students brainstorms and records possible resources—making an exhaustive list. (Remind students to include human resources, if appropriate.)

2. The teacher uses the "Process of Elimination" to record each group's list.

   A. The first group reads its entire list as the teacher writes the list on an overhead transparency.

   B. All other groups place checkmarks on their lists by any resources that the first group reads.

   C. The second group reads only those items that do not have a checkmark while other groups place checkmarks by those items on their lists that the second group reads.

   D. Continue until all groups have read items that have no checkmarks.

   E. The teacher adds any resources to the list that the groups omitted or resources that he or she wants to introduce to the class.

3. Discuss the prospects of each resource.

4. The teacher instructs each group to choose two to four from the overhead list that will best meet the needs of the task. (They may need to do this for each question being answered in the task, as not all resources will answer all questions.) Instruct each group to tell which ones it has chosen. Place check-marks beside each resource on the overhead as it is chosen. The ones with the most checkmarks will most likely be the resources that will be used for that assignment. (The teacher may direct groups to include particular ones—especially if he or she is introducing new or unknown resources to the class.) Groups should not be limited to the two to four resources chosen by the class, however. Some students will have additional valid resources available to them through friends and family.

The benefits of using the "Process of Exclusion" include (1) requiring students to listen to each other to avoid repetition when sharing results of brainstorming; (2) allowing the teacher to introduce new or previously unknown resources to students; (3) giving the teacher direction on where to begin or review instruction in using general or specific resources; and (4) giving students a focus for engaging in the assignment—they have a place to start and other resources to consult if the CD-ROM stations are in use!

Title: Which Is Best? Choosing the Resource for Me

Author: Barbara A. Jansen

Related Big6 Skills: Big6 #2–Information Seeking Strategies

Purpose: The purpose of this lesson is to introduce students to selecting resources.

Learning Contexts: This lesson is applicable across subjects with young students (grades 2–3) when introducing selection of resources.

Discussion: Young learners (grades 2–3) need direct guidance in selecting resources. This lesson will help students learn how to choose the better of two resources. Most kindergarten through third grade children are developmentally unable to distinguish appropriate resources from inappropriate resources. Educators will probably need to choose resources for them and model the process used. However, beginning in second or third grade, children should have an opportunity to learn how to analyze and choose appropriate resources.

Sample in Context: Second graders, anxious to begin locating answers to questions developed for their upcoming social studies project, waited for the library media specialist to begin the class. They knew they would be looking for basic information on the countries from the Cinderella stories they had read, such as the language, native cuisine, capital city, picture of the flag, continent, etc. The library media specialist (LMS) discussed the importance of choosing the best resource—Big6 #2. She talked about being able to quickly find basic information by reading chapter headings in books and subheadings in the encyclopedia as she displayed each on the overhead projector. She noted that the encyclopedia had the information in shorter paragraphs and the book had longer chapters. She then gave instructions for the following activity:

(Students should be in pairs—number each pair.) Half the pairs should have the appropriate encyclopedia and the other half should have an appropriate book. Each pair should have a ready reference question written on a slip of paper. The question should be similar to the one the students will find for the upcoming country project, such as "What language is spoken in India?" The answer should be available in their encyclopedia or book.

1. Pick up the sentence strip and read the question.

2. In the book you have been provided, find the answer to the question.

3. When you find the answer, stand up and go to the front of the room.

As each pair comes to the front, write its group number on the overhead or board. After all or most groups have been to the front, focus the class's attention on the overhead display. As you call each group number, ask the pair which resource it used, the book or encyclopedia. Write this beside each pair's number. Students should see that the encyclopedias were almost always at the top half of the list. Discuss using encyclopedias for many ready reference-type questions—those questions that have a "right" answer—one that doesn't have an opinion and is usually a supporting detail. Encyclopedias are useful for information that does not change or depend on regular updates. (Of course, this is not applicable for Web-based encyclopedias such as Britannica Online which is capable of daily updates.)

REFLECTIONS

CHAPTER 8

Big6™ Tips:
Location & Access—Think
Index, Keywords, and Boolean

Stage three of the Big6 process, **Location & Access**, has two components:

3.1 Locate sources.
3.2 Find information within sources.

Location & Access, the focus of most traditional "library skills" curricula, are clearly important skills. However, with the Big6 and other process-oriented approaches, we now recognize that Location & Access skills are part of a broader process. Once students understand their task and brainstorm and select the most appropriate source to use for the situation, it's now time to actually get the source and the relevant information from within the source.

In the Big6 approach, we like to think about Location & Access from a top-down perspective. That is, rather than jump into the details, we prefer to focus on the big concepts and skills. With Location & Access, for example, there's a tendency to get caught up with teaching the mechanics of search commands, the use of guide-

> *Librarians love indexes—and with good reason. Indexes are the key to effective and efficient information searching.*

words or other aids, or the features of an online catalog or database system. Certainly these aspects are important, but students first need to understand and appreciate the big picture.

For Location & Access that means the concept of **Index**. Say the word out loud—**Index**. Comforting, isn't it? Librarians love indexes—and with good reason. Indexes are the key to effective and efficient information searching. Indexes make it possible to find useful information in books, databases, and even in that most massive of information stores—the World Wide Web. So, before we work with students on skills related to the specific use of indexes, we first want them to appreciate and seek out indexes. Here's a sample exercise for teaching this—to have students recognize and value indexes:

Explain the concept of "index" to the class. Explain about sequential access to information—looking through a book page by page or browsing through a database record by record. Then explain the point of an index—an "inverted file" that organizes the content alphabetically for easy searching and location.

Show the class some common indexes—the index in the back of their science book, the library catalog, or the index to the encyclopedia. Make sure they understand the concept.

Now challenge them to identify indexes in everyday life. You give them the type of information, and they have to note the index. For example:

Telephone	– the phone book
Stores in a shopping mall	– the directory
Television shows	– the TV guide in the newspaper
Candy in a supermarket	– the videotext system.

There are plenty of these. Challenge them to stump you as well.

The point is to help students realize that if they really want to save time and effort in locating and accessing information—find the index. Another way to teach the idea of **Index** is to use the World Wide Web and search engines. Divide the class, but only let one group use a search engine, the other must browse; then switch. They will quickly see why Yahoo and the other search engines are so popular. You can expand on this by testing the different search engines. Have the class attempt to search for the same topic, but with different groups using different search engines. Let students set the criteria (number of hits, speed, ease-of-use, information displayed, etc.), run the tests, and make the comparisons. I've done this with students as young as fourth grade, and I was amazed at their insights.

A discussion of search engines often leads to considering search strategies and keywords. Using Indexes and keyword search strategies are both essential skills for Location & Access.

...Research shows that students rarely consider alternative terms when searching for information. They are more likely to change their topic than try synonyms!

However, research shows that students rarely consider alternative terms when searching for information. They are more likely to change their topic than try synonyms! So, discuss what a synonym is (you'll be amazed at what you hear), and try to get them to expand their thinking and brainstorm various alternatives to represent the topic they are seeking. Use graphic organizers (charts and mind maps) to facilitate brainstorming keywords.

Finally, there's the matter of Boolean searching. In electronic indexes, search results can be expanded by linking terms with a Boolean term, "or." Conversely, results can be narrowed with a Boolean term, "and." Students readily grasp these concepts when they are searching a magazine index or the Web. But remember the top-down approach: students are ready for learning about Boolean operators only after they fully grasp the concept of index and the value of keywords.

Title: Beginning, Middle, and End: Using the Alphabet to Introduce the Encyclopedia

Author: *Barbara A. Jansen*

Related Big6 Skills: *Big6 #3–Location & Access*

Purpose: *The purpose of this lesson is to help young learners quickly locate topics in an encyclopedia.*

Learning Contexts: This lesson is applicable across subject areas for young students (grades 2–3) and students with special learning needs.

Discussion: This lesson will introduce the encyclopedia to young learners. Young students should be directed in using an encyclopedia so the experience will be successful and not overwhelming.

Sample in Context: Second grade students will create a travel brochure about a trip to another planet. They will find facts about their planet, justify the reasons to travel to that planet, and explain what the traveler can do once there. Included will be a list of items that the travelers may want to bring with them, including proper attire and other important items to pack.

Activities (Research):

Day One (in classroom):

1. Librarian introduces the Big6 using Maybelle the Cow puppet (she is reciting "Hey, Diddle, Diddle") and stops at the part "the cow jumps over the moon." She questions why a cow would even want to do that. Then Maybelle starts thinking aloud about if the moon is really made of green cheese, and why, when she eats green grass, does she give white milk and not green. She then introduces her toolbox, the Big6, which she learned in first grade. Maybelle reads the poem (see Big6 Poetry, p. 76) about the Big6.

2. Librarian introduces Big6 #1–Task Definition (show transparency) and Maybelle reads the poem. The classroom teacher discusses the task and the information needed for the task.

3. Librarian introduces Big6 #2–Information Seeking Strategies (show transparency) and again, Maybelle reads the poem. Have the class quickly brainstorm all the possible ways it could find out the information to their questions. Then have them choose the most logical and best information sources.

Day Two (in library with fifth grade Research Buddies)

1. Maybelle introduces the class to Big6 #3–Location & Access (show transparency) and reads the poem. Each pair of students looks at their planet name and gets the corresponding encyclopedia. Look at the transparency of the alphabet and the second letter of the planet name. Write the alphabet on a transparency and divide the alphabet into thirds. Have the students choose the part (beginning, middle, or end) of the alphabet where the second letter falls. Tell them that they should open to either the beginning, middle, or close to the end of the encyclopedia to save time. Find the article about their planet (with teacher and librarian help as appropriate) and have pairs of students mark the beginning and end of the planet article with small Post-it™ notes.

2. Look at the subheadings and match key-words to information needed in Big6 #1.

3. Librarian and Maybelle introduce Big6 #4 the same way as above. Fifth grade Big6 Buddies help the second graders locate and record their information on the question sheets provided. Give the students an awareness that not all words are used unless the word is needed to answer Big6 #1.

4. When finished, have Maybelle show transparencies of Big6 #5 and explain to the students that they will use the information about the planets to make a travel brochure as defined in Big6 #1.

5. In the classroom, the librarian will guide the class in using the Primary evaluation sheet (See "What Did I Learn," p. 123), when they are finished with their products. Show Big6 #6 transparency and read the poem.

Evaluation: The teacher will use a scoring rubric to assess the final product and the librarian will guide students through the primary evaluation sheet to self-evaluate.

Big6 Poetry
Written by Barbara A. Jansen

When I have something that needs to be done,
And I need information because I have none.
I'll use my tools that help me do
The job that I'm happy to share with you.
The Big6 will help me find what I need,
And put it together, I can do it, indeed!

When I have a task, that is something to do,
And I need information to do it because it is new,
Big6 #1 will help me succeed
By figuring out just what exactly I need.

Big6 #2 will help me choose
When I decide just what I can use.
I'll choose the ones that meet my needs best,
I may choose two or three and leave all the rest.

Where, oh, where can I find these things now?
In the library? In a book? And Big6 #3 tells just how
To find those people or print that I choose,
And get to where my information is located in those.

Read, look, and listen is what I'll do when
I use Big6 #4 to get just what I need and then
I'll write it or draw the information I find.
I'll get what I need because I'll use my mind.

Once I have found and written all that I need,
I must put it together so I can proceed
To finish the job and show it, you see,
And Big6 #5 will surely help me.

How will I know if I did my job well?
Big6 #6 will sure help me to tell
If I did it the best that I possibly could,
And do it better the next time if I should.

Big6 ©Michael B. Eisenberg and Robert E. Berkowitz, 1990
Words to song and poetry © Barbara A. Jansen, 1994.

Title: The Key to Understanding: Using Keywords and Related Words for Location & Access

Author: *Barbara A. Jansen*

Related Big6 Skills: *Big6 #3–Location & Access*

Purpose: *The purpose of this lesson is to help students make the connection between the information they need and the information that is in the source they have selected.*

Learning Contexts: This lesson is applicable across subject areas in elementary settings (grades 3–5) where students are learning how to access information.

Discussion: In this lesson, teachers will help students learn to identify keywords and related words. Due to the varied terminology and vocabulary used, many elementary students have difficulty making the connection between the information needed and the information presented in a book or article they select. The students' natural language (as written in the questions they developed in Big6 #1.2) will certainly differ from the language in a source. Students' limited vocabulary and experience with reading for information may impede their efforts in finding relevant information. Identifying keywords and listing related words will help students find relevant information. This exercise "unlocks" the meaning in the sentence and provides additional access points.

Sample in Context: The teacher or librarian will explain the terms "keyword" or "key phrase" before demonstrating this procedure to the students. Students should participate in the discussion while the teacher or librarian demonstrates the procedure. For example, you may ask, "What is this question really asking?" and then underline the important word or words.

Have students look at the questions they wrote for Big6 #1.2. Students should underline the important words (keywords or phrases) in each question. Once students understand what is required, this process seems simple.

Students should write related words beside or under the keywords. The teacher or librarian will check students' work and give suggestions as needed, due to the students' limited vocabulary. This is a good time to introduce the thesaurus or synonym finder.

Demonstrate how knowing keywords and related words can help when searching for information in the source. Instruct students to look for these words when they are searching for information.

Title: Madeline: Fact or Fiction?

Author: *Tami J. Little (original lesson idea by Jane Roder)*

Related Big6 Skills: *Big6 #3–Location & Access, and Big6 #4–Use of Information*

Purpose: *The purpose of this lesson is to show students that the story settings in fiction books can sometimes be a real place.*

Learning Contexts: This lesson can demonstrate that facts are often found in fiction books.

Discussion: Often times, students reading fiction books think that the stories are all fiction. Students can discover that real people who have been to real places write fiction books. The setting for the book *Madeline* by Ludwig Bemelmans is Paris, France.

The librarian will read *Madeline* aloud and will ask the children if they know the name of the tower that is on the cover of the *Madeline* book. (It is the Eiffel Tower.) Then the librarian will ask if the book is fact or fiction. From the discussion, students will discover that although the story is fiction, there are some pictures of real monuments, museums, and historical places in Paris, France. The librarian will page through the book, asking students to determine if each illustration could be a "real" monument, museum, or historical place.

The librarian will then ask the students to determine (Big6 #2) some possible sources for locating the real pictures. Sources will be such things as the Internet, the encyclopedia, books from the library, travel agency, or a person in the community who has traveled to France, etc.

Location & Access

- Students will use the encyclopedia to attempt to locate the names of places they see.
- Students will access non-fiction books about France in the library.
- Students will use the Internet search engine *http://www.yahooligans.com/* to find information about France.

Use of Information

- Students will complete an Internet scavenger hunt (see the sample), Madeline: Fact or Fiction?

To assess the activity, students will create a book of their own with drawings or printouts of the pages for each of the following: the Eiffel Tower, Le Louvre, Palais Royal, Hôtel des Invalides, and the Tuleries Garden. Advanced students can label or write a sentence about each of the monuments, museums, or historic places.

Follow-up could include students doing research on one or more of the monuments, museums, or historical places in France. Other activities could include having Madeline travel to another country and drawing realistic backdrops for her trip. Students could research French foods and have a celebration that includes authentic French cuisine.

In language class, students could learn some simple French words such as please, thank you, and good-bye. Students could also experiment with rhyming as the book is written in rhyme.

There is a movie about Madeline, released in theatres in July 1998. Students could view the movie and discuss the similarities and differences between the books and the movie.

Communicate with parents about the *Madeline* lesson. Encourage parents to participate in an information search for extension activities. Ask if any parents have traveled to another country. Invite parents with expertise or experience to come share with the class. (See the sample letter to parents.)

Dear Parent(s),

The fourth grade students recently participated in the Big6 Information Skills lesson, Madeline: Fact or Fiction. In this lesson, the students discovered that *Madeline*, the children's book by Ludwig Bemelmans, is about a young girl who lived in France. Madeline was an orphan who attended a church boarding school. The backdrop for the book contains illustrations for monuments, a museum, and historical places in France.

You can access the Web site and see the same information from your home or the public library. With your child, see the French flag *http://fotw.digibel.be/images/fr.gif*. Visit the French Embassy in Washington, D.C., online: *http://www.info-france-usa.org/*

■ Take a tour of Paris at: *http://sunsite.unc.edu/wm/paris/tour/*
■ See the Eiffel Tower at: *http://www.tour-eiffel.fr/tour_uk/*
■ View a map of France and read history, facts, and more than you would ever need to know about France at: *http://www.odci.gov/cia/publications/factbook/fr.html*
■ See detailed pictures of Paris at: *http://www.paris.org/*

When you are using the Internet with your child, review the Internet Safety Rules that you have established in your home. If you have not established rules yet and would like some guidance, feel free to call me at school and I will be happy to give you some suggestions.

Have you visited Paris? Do you know someone who has? The students are interested in asking questions of someone who has seen Paris! Please contact me at school if you are interested in presenting information to the class.

For extension activities, visit another country or city "virtually," use the encyclopedia, or check the public library. Help your child decide which places would be most interesting for Madeline to visit.

Perhaps Madeline will visit Chicago? New York? Spain? Canada?

Sincerely,

Mrs. Little

Madeline: Fact or Fiction
Internet Scavenger Hunt

Directions: Locate the Web pages listed below. Find the pictures described.
Print the pictures as you find them.

On the cover of the book *Madeline* is an illustration of a famous tower in Paris, France.
Visit the site: *http://www.tour-eiffel.fr/tour_uk/*

What is the name of the tower?

What can you see if you visit the tower?

Who built the tower?

Visit the site: *http://www.paris.org/*
- Find the picture of the Opera where the girls "smiled at the good."
- Find the picture of the Place Vendome where the girls "frowned at the bad."
- Find the picture of the Hotel Des Invalides where the girls "were very sad."
- Find the picture of Notre Dame where the girls were "in the rain."
- Find the picture of the sunny day where the girls were looking across the Gardens at the Luxembourg.
- Find the picture of the Church of the Sacre Coeur where the girls are skating in the "winter, snow and ice."
- Find the picture of the bridge that Madeline likes to walk across to frighten Miss Clavel.
- Find the picture of the Tuileries Garden that is facing the Louvre on the page that Miss Clavel said, "Isn't this a fine"— A man is feeding birds on the park bench.

Describe three to five new things you learned about France from viewing the Web pages.

Would you like to visit Madeline in France? Tell why or why not.

REFLECTIONS

REFLECTIONS

CHAPTER 9

Big6™ Tips: Use of Information – Where the Rubber Meets the Road

Stage four of the Big6 process is Use of Information. **Use of Information** has two components:

4.1 Engage (read, hear, view) the information in a source.
4.2 Extract relevant information.

Use of Information marks a major shift in focus in the information problem-solving process. Previously, most of the Big6 action revolved around finding information sources to match information needs. But now, things change—from selecting and accessing sources to using information itself. This is "where the rubber meets the road" because it requires heavy-duty "critical thinking" as students engage the information in a source (Ann Irving from England calls this "interrogating an information source") in order to recognize relevant information (Big6 #4.1). The challenge is to extract the relevant information through some form of note-taking.

Engaging information involves reading and media comprehension and is the heart of what we

The challenge is to extract the relevant information through some form of note-taking.

mean by literacy. This is a major concern of classroom teachers, particularly language arts and reading teachers. However, teacher-librarians can also help students learn effective Use of Information skills by working with students on:

■ Recognizing where comprehension fits in the overall information problem-solving process
■ Skimming and scanning techniques, and
■ Identifying relevant information.

For example, relevance is more than simply "being on a topic." There are degrees of relevance based on the original charge (Task Definition) and how the student will present the result (Synthesis). In her dissertation on user criteria of relevance, Carol Barry (1994) found that people base relevance decisions on: recency, depth/scope, accuracy, clarity, and novelty. Here's a technique for teaching students to recognize and apply relevance criteria:

Before students are about to use information resources related to their own tasks, give students an information problem and a one-page reading that addresses that problem. Ask them to highlight the passages that they think are relevant to the problem. Then ask them to go back and explain why they selected the passages. Compare their reasons to Barry's criteria. Finally, using a different colored highlighter, have them go over the reading again. You may want to do this more than once before having the students begin working on their own tasks.

For younger students, take a look at Barbara Jansen's "Trash-N-Treasure" technique (Jansen, 1997, 1996 and p. 93 in this book). It's a highly useful Big6-related approach to help younger students learn to engage and extract relevant information.

It is also important to assess whether students are able to engage and identify relevant information before we ask them to extract, combine, and present information. This isn't always clear in schools. For example, when completing a typical homework assignment—answering questions at the end of a chapter—we ask students to answer the question in their own words. That's fine, but what we are really doing is asking them to locate, access, engage, extract, organize, and present—that's Big6 numbers 3 through 5 all at once! If they get the wrong answer, how do you know if the problem was in getting to the right place in the textbook (Big6 #3) or understanding the content (Big6 #4) or writing the answer in their own words (Big6 #5). I believe you've got to "walk before you can run." So, try this:

Early in the school year, just focus on engage (Big6 #4.1) and extract (Big6# 4.2). When the students are doing that typical homework assignment, forget about putting the answer in their own words. Put the answer in direct quotes and cite the page(s) where the quote appears. That will help classroom teachers and teacher-librarians assess whether students are able to comprehend the information (engage) and identify the relevant sections (extract). Later, the students can work on using their own words,

...The note-card method is actually not designed for efficient note-taking—it's designed for efficient organization of information after all the notes are available.

the Synthesis part.

The point is to go beyond simply expecting students to be able to comprehend and use information. Classroom teachers, librarians, and reading specialists need to work together to help students improve their ability to sift through lots of information and recognize what's relevant to their specific task, problem, or need.

After developing Big6 #4.1–Engage (read, hear, view) the information in a source, we need to pay specific attention to Big6 #4.2–Extract relevant information.

Librarians and classroom teachers have taught classic note-taking skills for many years. This usually involves some form of the "note-card" method—writing single ideas from a source on a 3x5 card along with a notation that links the card to the full citation for the source. Information about the sources is usually stored on cards as well—the bibliography cards.

Why teach the note-card method? Is it an efficient way to take notes from a source? If teacher-librarians were asked to write a scholarly paper on some topic, would they use the note-card method themselves? Probably not. That's because the note-card method is actually not designed for efficient note-taking—it's designed for efficient organization of information *after* all the notes are available. Therefore, note-cards help with Big6 Skill #5.1–organization of information, not #4.2–extraction.

That's not to say we should abandon the note-card method. It just means that we should be clear about our reasons for using the method. The key to the note-card method is this business of using only one card per main idea, point, or concept. If students write more than one idea on a card, they've defeated the whole purpose for using the method. But, students often do write more than one idea on a card because they don't want to "waste" space on cards! So, it's critical to make sure students understand the purpose of the note-cards if they are going to use this method.

But, let's consider alternatives to the note-card method. Again, what would you do if you were given the task of extracting information for a scholarly paper? Well, in college, most of us probably used some form of the "photocopy-highlight" method of extraction of information. We went to the library and used the catalog or periodical indexes to identify relevant books and journal articles (Big6 Skills #3.1), located the important sections in the books and articles (Big6 Skills #3.2), and took a quick look to make sure that the sections contained what we wanted (Big6 #4.1). Then we made photocopies of all the pages we wanted to use. That's extraction of information—Big6 #4.2. We would also make sure that we noted the full citation of the source on the front page of the photocopied page. Later, we would go back and read the copies in detail (Big6 #4.1), highlighting specific sections that we wanted to use (Big6 #4.2). And finally, we would use some method for taking that information and organizing it for our paper (Big6 #5.1). This might involve marking up the highlighted sections using some form of coding scheme related to the outline of our paper or rewriting the notes according to a draft outline of the paper (Big6 #5.2). Today, most of us would use word processing software to assist with this endeavor.

We talk about the changing information landscape so let's make sure our students are prepared for it.

Computer-based information resources and processing capabilities offer new opportunities and challenges for Use of Information and Synthesis. For example, many teachers and teacher-librarians complain that all the students do is print out everything—without even thinking about whether they are going to use the information. Let's look at this more carefully. First, there may be good reasons for printing out everything; perhaps there are only a few limited computer stations and other students want to use them. Second, reading text on a screen can become tedious. You try it—would you rather read page after page on the screen or print it out and read it later? Lastly, printing out is not all that different from photocopying—except we were paying by the page so we took some time to make sure that the sections we copied were ones we wanted to use. So, let's do the same with students—have them quickly skim the screen to make sure the sections they are printing are relevant to their needs.

We also need to follow-up on techniques for highlighting and organizing the information once it is printed out. How about offering instruction on identifying relevant information within text. Give all students the same article, highlighters, and a topic to study. See what they highlight and if they agree. Chances are they will highlight too much. So work on this with more examples and different colored highlighters. Also help students learn how to work totally on the computer—going from an online source, to highlight and copy on screen, to paste into a word processing program. Having a rough outline of the paper in advance can greatly enhance this process, and don't forget to work with them on time-saving techniques of keeping track of citations for the sections they copied and pasted.

Students also need to learn how to extract relevant information from other forms of information besides print and electronic. Consider offering lessons (always in the context of real assignments and curriculum) in relation to human sources (interview note-taking, audio recording), television (video recording), observation (photography, video recording, field notes), and other forms of multimedia. We talk about the changing information landscape so let's make sure our students are prepared for it.

Title: Big6 Buddies

Author: Barbara A. Jansen

Related Big6 Skills: All Big6 Skills with a focus on Big6 #1–Task Definition, Big6 #5–Synthesis, and Big6 #4–Use of Information.

Purpose: The purpose of this lesson is to introduce young learners to the Big6 process.

Learning Contexts: This lesson is applicable (grades K–2) where young learners are not developmentally ready to read and take notes but the teacher and librarian want them to become aware of the process.

Discussion: In this lesson, older students (Big6 Buddies) take notes for young learners. Young learners are not developmentally capable of searching for and extracting information independently. However, these young students become aware that the Big6 process is useful when they need to gather information. Since young students are capable of using the information, but cannot read and take notes independently, have older students help them with Big6 #2–Information Seeking Strategies, Big6 #3–Location & Access, and especially Big6 #4–Use of Information. This is a successful way to get the information that young students need to use for a product. Teachers and librarians can even have the information sources selected and located to save time with the older students (the Big6 Buddies) accessing the information, reading aloud, and taking notes for the younger students. Students in grades one and two can even begin to do some of the writing with the assistance of the Big6 Buddies. The older students have opportunities to practice note-taking and have a sense of accomplishment and worth by helping their "Little Buddies." Older students take this responsibility seriously and are successful with the task. The teacher and librarian need to dis-cuss ahead of time with the older students the importance and the requirements of the task. Tell them that they should read the question aloud, then read aloud the passage from the information source that "answers" the question. They should stop and ask the Little Buddy how that section helps answer the question. If the young student does not respond appropriately, the Big6 Buddy should tell him why it answers the question, then write the appropriate notes in words that the young student can understand.

Once the notes are taken, the young students can have parents or teachers assist with the final product, or students can begin to synthesize the information for themselves on a developmentally appropriate product.

Sample in Context:

Big6 #1–Task Definition: First grade teachers will explain to the students that they will learn about cowhands and choose how they want to share the information they discover. Students devise several questions they would need to know if they were to become a cowhand. (Teachers and librarians will devise a set of questions. Possible questions:

- What kind of gear do cowhands need?
- What kind of clothes do they wear and for what is each used?
- What are the dangers to cowhands?
- Where do cowhands live and sleep on a ranch and trail drive?

- What do they need?
- What do cowhands eat and where do they get their food?

Write questions on a modified data chart for fifth grade Big6 Buddies to use with their first grade Little Buddies.

Pair fifth graders with first graders and hand out prepared data charts.

The librarian reviews the task and the questions that are on the data chart. Then the librarian reviews with the fifth graders how they will read aloud to their Little Buddies the sections that contain the information they seek, and have them listen for the "answers" to the identified questions on the data chart. Big6 Buddies will write the notes in words first graders can understand and cite the source. The Little Buddies should be instructed to pay close attention to their Big6 Buddies and to listen for answers to the questions on the data chart.

Big6 #2–Information Seeking Strategies: Tell students that this is done for them—choose encyclopedias (print and CD-ROM) and books.

Big6 #3–Location & Access: Information sources will be available for students to use. Tell students that sources are already pulled off the shelves and ready for use. Fifth grade students will access encyclopedia articles in print and CD-ROM.

Big6 #4–Use of Information: Fifth grade Big6 Buddies will help first graders find information, take notes, and cite sources.

Big6 #5–Synthesis: Students use *KidPix*, a multimedia program, to create "slide" illustrations of the located information. Students can illustrate and record the information they've located. Traditional print and drawing projects can also be created. Teachers, Big6 Buddies, and parents can help the young students with the planning and technical production.

Sharing products or performances: Invite Big6 Buddies to classrooms to eat cowhand fare and share products.

Big6 #6–Evaluation: Teachers guide students through the informal written evaluation sheet about the project and students fill in answers to questions.

Title: Science and the Big6

Author: Barbara A. Jansen

Related Big6 Skills: All Big6 Skills with a focus on Big6 #4–Use of Information, Big6 #5–Synthesis, and Big6 #6–Evaluation

Purpose: The purpose of this lesson is to integrate e-mail, database, and student-designed products into the science curriculum.

Learning Contexts: This lesson is applicable in science (grades 5–6) where teachers and librarians want to integrate information skills, technology, and science content.

Discussion: In this lesson, students study rocks and minerals in preparation for a science lab. Students often need to locate background information. If the Big6 is used, students have a systematic way to find and present the information for the lab, just as they use the scientific method to systematically experiment in the science lab. When students are required to teach each other what they have learned, they tend to understand the content better. Having a peer audience for their presentations motivates them to put effort into the product.

Sample in Context: Focus students' attention by asking what they like to do on the weekends. Use the scenario of buying an object (bike) to introduce the Big6 Skills. Ask what they should know about bikes before they buy a new one. Have groups list where they could find this information about bikes. The librarian writes on an overhead transparency (no illumination at this point). Use the "exclusion" technique to avoid duplication. (When groups hear, from another group, an item called out that is on their list, they place a checkmark by it. Then when it is their turn, they read only those items that do not have check marks.) After the librarian goes through steps #3–#6 orally, she applies them to the Big6, using the Big6 transparencies.

Display the student-generated list on Big6 Skill #2. When finished, relate this process to the Texas rocks and minerals database (which is their immediate assignment).

Introduce Big6 #1 and #2–Task Definition and Information Seeking Strategies.

With the science teacher, present Big6 Skill #1–Task Definition; define the task for the class. Inform the class that the task is defined by their teachers, but many times they will have to do it themselves. Then introduce Big6 #2–Information Seeking Strategies. In groups, have students list every person, place, or print resource they can think of to find the information specified in the Task Definition. List these on the overhead, using the "exclusion" technique to avoid repetition. Then have each group choose two or three resources that they would consider the best. They should circle or otherwise note their choices and be able to justify their decisions. The librarian will place checkmarks on these on the overhead.

Introduce Big6 #3–Location & Access.

The librarian will, in the context of the Big6, work through Big6 #3 (remind students to use the table of contents and indices) quickly showing index entries and card catalog information. Briefly discuss the phone book arrangement, as appropriate to groups.

Students locate available resources in the library media center and make a list for later citation and retrieval. The resources should answer their questions about their assigned topic.

Introduce Big6 #4–Use of Information.

Tell students that they will use data charts to record pertinent pieces of information. Review "trash and treasure" words and methods of extracting relevant information. *Guided practice:* On the overhead, show an excerpt of a scientific article about a prehistoric animal. On the overhead, show a question that must be answered. Have students use a data chart to record the least amount of information that they can that satisfies the information need identified in the question. Review citing procedures. Students use a list compiled from day two to locate and extract information from sources.

Introduce Big6 Skills #5 and #6– Synthesis and Evaluation.

Have each group generate a list of components that a good presentation should include (part of their evaluation of effectiveness Big6 #6.1). Write (using exclusion) the list on the overhead and create a custom list for each of the four classes to use when designing a presentation. The science teacher will use the computer to generate the checklist, print it, and give one to each group.

Give each group a piece of paper on which to take notes as the group talks about ideas. Students list what each member does well, strengths and talents. Groups must ensure that everyone is included in planning and presenting, and try to use everyone's talent. Get approval from the teacher or librarian. List the materials needed. (The teacher and librarian will confer with each group as they are making decisions.) The librarian and teacher will help the students organize their notes into categories.

The librarian and teacher will assist the students in creating their presentations (skit, video, puppet play, etc.) to present to the other classmates. Each group presents its topic to the other groups in the class instructional setting. The students will be responsible for taking notes on the information presented.

The language arts teachers will assist each group in completing a page of a booklet about rocks, minerals, and the geology of the area to include with the earth science materials in the science lab and library media collection. This booklet can be used by other classes studying rocks and minerals as well as fifth grade classes in subsequent years.

Big6 #6–Evaluation.

Group products and presentations will be evaluated using a rubric which the class has helped construct. This will include both the product and the process. Students also complete an informal written evaluation of their individual process and product.

Students will conduct experimentation in the science lab on unidentified rocks and minerals native to the county and build a database that will be used by future classes in rock study.

Science I Presentation List

Planning: The Presentation Must Include These Things:

1. Information about the topic (details)
2. Visuals—something to see
3. Examples of rocks
4. Involvement for presenter and audience
5. Conclusion (ending, warm-up)
6. Include questions for evaluation

During Our Presentation We Should Do These Things:

1. Have a clear and enthusiastic voice tone
2. Look at the audience
3. Speak in whole sentences
4. Move around the room, don't stand in one spot
5. Dress in a nice way the day of the presentation

Science I Presentation Evaluation

Presentation Content:

Information about the topic (details)—separate content grade

_____Visual _____

_____Examples of rocks_____

_____Involvement for presenter and audience_____

_____Conclusion _____

_____Include questions for evaluation _____

Presentation:

_____Have a clear and enthusiastic voice tone

_____Look at the audience

_____Speak in whole sentences

_____Move around the room don't stand in one spot

_____Dress in a nice way the day of the presentation

Group members:

_____

_____

_____

_____

_____

_____

Total points: _____

Presentation grade (points X 5): _____

Explanation of points:

0 = Criteria not present

1 = Criteria partially present

2 = Criteria present

Rocks and Minerals

Big6™ Number Six—Evaluation   **Due:** _____

Name: _____

Topic: _____

Circle one: Science   1   2   3   4

Now that you have finished the first part of our Rocks and Minerals Database Project by presenting information on rocks or minerals to your classmates, it is time to think about what you have accomplished. Please think about what you learned and the steps you followed in order to make your presentation. Write an evaluation of this experience, including the following:

Your contribution to your group in finding information for the data chart and in preparing the presentation
Your participation with your group
What you learned (about the science content and in working with others)
What you did well
What you would do differently next time

Please rate yourself on a scale of zero to ten (zero is low and ten is high)
My contribution to the think cards _____
My contribution to the presentation _____

Use the space below and on the back to write your self-evaluation.

Title: "Trash-N-Treasure" Approach to Teaching Note-Taking

Author: *Barbara A. Jansen*

Related Big6 Skills: *Big6 #4–Use of Information*

Purpose: *The purpose of this lesson is to help students discriminate between needed and superfluous information when taking notes.*

Learning Contexts: This lesson is applicable across subject areas in elementary school (grades 3–6) when students are learning how to take notes.

Discussion: In this lesson, students learn to take notes by example. How often do we say, "don't copy out of the encyclopedia" to young learners, but fail to teach them otherwise? Young learners have difficulty identifying and extracting appropriate information from the vast amount of text that may appear in an informational article and really have no other choice than to copy. Unless taught, they have no concept of what is relevant to their needs and what is not. By directly teaching knowledge-level note-taking, students will be able to critically analyze information for relevancy and validity, writing only that which meets identified needs. It takes time and practice to develop this skill. As students mature and are able to think abstractly, they will be able to take notes at a higher level such as paraphrasing, drawing conclusions, and making inferences from the information located.

Sample in Context: Try relating note-taking to a pirate's treasure map! (Show an example of a treasure map, if necessary). The map itself is like the article or chapter of a book containing information about the topic. The "X" on the treasure map, which marks the exact location of the buried treasure, is the section of the text containing needed information, or an "answer" for specific questions defined in the task. A pirate must dig for the treasure chest and toss aside dirt, weeds, rocks, and trash. A researcher must also dig to find words that help answer the questions—treasure words. He or she must "toss aside" unnecessary sentences, phrases, and words—trash words. Of course, these words are not trash to the original source, only to the researcher because they do not answer the questions defined in the task.

Demonstrate this concept using an overhead projector and transparency of an encyclopedia article or section. The students should each have a copy of the article so they can follow along and practice the technique. Show a prepared question, including the underlined keywords and a list of related words. Scan the article until the appropriate heading is located. Place a slash at the end of the first sentence and read it. Ask, "Does this sentence answer the question?" If the answer is no, tell the students that sentence is "trash" to them. Go on to the next sentence, placing a slash at the end. If the answer is yes, underline the first phrase and ask if that phrase answers the question. If the answer is no, underline the next phrase and repeat the question. If the answer is yes, read that phrase word by word, asking which words are needed to answer the question—these are treasure words. Circle those words, then write them in the appropriate place on the overhead data chart or whichever organizer the students are using. (See below for directions for constructing and using a data chart.) Words that do not answer the question are trash words. Continue phrase-by-phrase and word-by-word until reaching the end of the sentence.

Count the words in the sentence and then count the treasure words. Students are very impressed when you say, "The sentence has 17 words and I only needed to write four of them. I don't know about you, but I would rather write four than 17!"

Demonstrate the process again, allowing the students to practice, using copies of the article. Allow students to independently practice a few times before they begin their own research. The library media specialist and teacher should monitor each student's work, re-teaching as necessary. Don't expect mastery at the elementary grades; just expect students to gain proficiency as they have opportunities to practice this skill.

Of course, students will not be able to slash, underline, and circle the original article. If you have access to a copy machine, make photocopies of the article so students can practice the skill. Otherwise, students will need to understand the concept and take treasure notes with their brains, eyes, and pencils.

Directions for constructing and using a data chart

Have students fold a legal size sheet of paper (or larger) into 16 boxes. In the upper-left box, students write their name and topic. The other boxes in the top row are used for writing questions to be answered (one question per box). The two middle boxes in the first column are used to cite sources, and the box at the bottom of the first column is for the summary. This makes a grid—questions across the top, sources down the side. If the students use more than one source, make the paper larger or tape some more rows onto the bottom. The "answers" to the questions are written in a box under the appropriate question, on the same row as the source that answered it. The last row is saved for a summary (Big6 #5.1) of the information that multiple sources gave about a single question.

Name: Topic:	Question #1	Question #2	Question #3
Source #1	Answer:	Answer:	Answer:
Source #2	Answer:	Answer:	Answer:
	Summary:	Summary:	Summary:

REFLECTIONS

REFLECTIONS

CHAPTER 10

The BIG 6

Big6™ Tips: Synthesis— Putting It All Together

This TIP focuses on the Big6 #5–**Synthesis**— bringing all the information elements together to show what you've learned. In the Synthesis stage, researchers will do the following:

5.1 Organize information from multiple sources.
5.2 Present the result.

Synthesis is the result, the output part of the information process. It's also the most visible part of the process. And, synthesis takes place in every information problem-solving situation. Yes, synthesis includes writing a research paper or report or creating some form of project. But, synthesis is also:

- Answering multiple choice, fill-in, or short answer questions on a test

- Writing an essay, short story, or poem

- Creating a poster, overhead transparency, audiotape, TV show, multimedia presentation, or Web page

When people speak about the information explosion, they are talking about being overwhelmed by the amount and forms of synthesis.

- Making a decision (e.g., what college to attend, which product to buy, whether to invest in a stock or mutual fund, where to go for dinner), or

- Communicating in person, writing, telephone, via e-mail, chat, or videoconferencing.

All these are forms of synthesis for individuals or small groups. On the societal level we have synthesis through communications and mass media—television, radio, books, magazines, newspapers, videos, CD music, computer games and simulations, and, of course, the Internet and WWW. Synthesis is certainly a big part of our society. When people speak about the information explosion, they are talking about being overwhelmed by the amount and forms of synthesis.

As noted, from a Big6 perspective, Synthesis includes two aspects—organizing information and then presenting it. According to

Wurman (1989) in *Information Anxiety*, there are a number of ways to organize information:

- By category (and subcategory)
- As a continuum (small to large or low to high, or the reverse)
- Alphabetically
- By time
- As a story (from beginning to end)
- Or as any combination of the above.

One interesting organizing (Big6 #5.1) activity to do with people of all ages is to bring in a collection of some kind (e.g., a music CD collection) and have groups decide how they would organize it. Also, ask them about various collections that they have—videos, toys, books, and dolls—and how they organize them. See if you can tease out the various options noted above for organizing information without having to present them yourself.

My favorite Big6 #5.1 exercise is to break a class into groups of five or so and give each group a manila envelope with 15 or so pictures in it. The pictures were cut from old magazines and are placed in no particular order, but I don't tell the groups that, of course. The task for each group is to organize the pictures in some way so they "make sense to them," to give the set of pictures a title, and to explain to the rest of the class how they organized the pictures. This leads to an entertaining session that usually results in some groups organizing by categories (e.g., people, places, and things), others develop a storyline around the pictures (e.g., a day in the life of...), and various other combinations of approaches. I always give as little direction as possible. In particular, I will only answer a key question if asked: "Do we have to use all the pictures?" My answer is rhetorical: "When we gather information for a project or report, do we have to use all the information that we find?" Clearly not.

Teaching forms of presenting, Big6 #5.2, is as important as working on organizing information. For example, consider the types of synthesis products that most students complete—homework, handouts, tests and quizzes, papers, and projects. One Big6 tip is to have students consider alternatives from a checklist when faced with presenting— alternatives in terms of time and effort as well as effectiveness in relation to the task. There's an important link between Synthesis and Task Definition, and I often suggest discussing "what the result should look like" as part of Task Definition and remembering, "what was the original purpose" as part of Synthesis.

Technology also plays a big role in synthesis. Think about all the computer software intended to help people present ideas and information: word processing, desktop publishing, graphic programs, audio/video editing, *PowerPoint* and presentation software, electronic spreadsheets, and even databases. Synthesis is a major industry in the world because you can have the best ideas, solutions, or insights in the world, but if you can't express them you are nowhere.

Therefore, it makes sense to integrate teaching software for Synthesis in the context of the Big6 process and real curriculum or personal needs. Students are highly motivated, and it is easy to demonstrate how they can save time and effort—and do a better job—by using technology in meaningful, contextual ways.

Synthesis is a major industry in the world because you can have the best ideas, solutions, or insights in the world, but if you can't express them you are nowhere.

Title: Celebrate 100th Day

Author: *Tami J. Little (original lesson plan ideas used with permission from J. De Jong)*

Related Big6 Skills: *Big6 #1–Task Definition, Big6 #5–Synthesis*

Purpose: *The purpose of this lesson is to teach students the concept of 100, and to identify e-mail as a communication tool.*

Learning Contexts: This lesson is applicable across the early childhood curriculum with activities for math, language arts, social studies, technology, and physical education.

Discussion: In this lesson, students will celebrate 100th Day by collecting 100 e-mail messages from 100 schools worldwide. The 100th Day Celebration is a tradition for students in many early childhood classrooms. Students record the first day of school and each day thereafter, practicing counting skills from day one through 100. For the 100th Day Celebration, students bring to school 100 items that fit in a baggie (provided by the teacher). Students count the 100 items they brought to school. Students write the numbers 1–100.

Possible curriculum connections include counting and writing to 100, classifying, and estimating for math. For language arts, the students enjoy a variety of books, write stories, and communicate ideas. The physical education teacher might have the students perform 100 exercises.

For a technology connection, students receive and mail a class e-mail. For social studies, the students and librarian place markers on a map showing from where the e-mails were sent.

Identify e-mail as a communication tool. Use the 100 e-mail messages to put markers on a map showing from where the messages were sent. The librarian invites the students to the library to watch as she sends a message to a list group requesting 100th Day Celebration greetings (see the sample). The librarian discusses e-mail as a tool for communication.

Sample Celebrate 100th Day E-mail Message:

Hello from Hinton Community School, Hinton, Iowa USA!

The first grade students in our school are going to have a 100th Day Celebration. We would love to have e-mail messages from 100 schools around the world so that we can see what a powerful communication tool e-mail is in the world. We have a map of the world on a bulletin board in our library. We are going to label each city from which we receive e-mail messages. Please send a message to the "reply to" address. In the subject line, please write "Celebrate 100th Day." In the body of the message, please tell us who wrote the letter as well as the name of the school, address, city, state, and zip code. Please also tell us if you celebrate Day 100 in your school.

Thank you so much for taking the time to send us an e-mail greeting.

Sincerely,

The First Grade Students
Hinton Community School
Hinton, Iowa USA

The students return to their classroom to read books about 100.

After several e-mails are received, the librarian prints them. A large bulletin board display is created of the United States (possibly the world). The students and the librarian use thumbtacks to place labels on a map showing from where the e-mails were received. This is a Synthesis activity showing the students that e-mail is a means for receiving 100 communications from around the United States (or world).

Plans for Integrated Instruction:

Teacher will:

1. Conduct preceding activities.
2. Read books.
3. Review estimation.

Librarian will:

1. Set up a class e-mail address for the first grade classrooms.
2. Send an e-mail to another class, listserv, or bulletin board telling about the 100th Day Celebration.
3. Receive, organize, create tags or labels for each city from which the e-mails arrive, and display the 100 e-mails.

Physical Education Teacher will:

1. Give instructions for 100 exercises. 10 jumping jacks, 10 hops on one foot, 10 knee-bends, etc.

Evaluation:

The students will evaluate the understanding of the use of 100 in life skills (orally).

The teacher will evaluate the stories, projects, and worksheets.

The librarian will evaluate the understanding of e-mail as a method of communication.

Sample in Context:

The 100th Day Celebration was so much fun for the children. The teachers created hats with green bands and a reproduction of a 100-dollar bill. The students loved wearing the hats to the lunchroom. There have always been many 100th Day activities, but the change this school year was the addition of the 100 e-mails lesson. The students were fascinated by the variety of e-mails and the locations from which they were sent. To see Hinton, Iowa, on the map and then to place a marker on the city in South Africa showed them far more than if they were just told that they received a message. The students were able to see the entire map full of markers and realize what a powerful tool e-mail is for communication.

For follow-up, the first grade students requested that they become class pen pals with another first grade classroom who also held a 100th Day Celebration. The students decided that they would each write a paper copy of a letter to be sent via surface mail, but the student of the week would be allowed to help with the e-mail letter. Students enjoyed the correspondence so much that they continued to send e-mail messages for the remainder of the school year.

Web Resources:

Web site: 150 Celebration Ideas. (Online) Available: *http://users.aol.com/aïday/ ideas. html 7/10/98.*

Bibliography:

Arnold, Tedd. (1995). *Five Ugly Monsters.* Scholastic.

Brown, Richard. (1987). *100 Words About Transportation.* Harcourt Brace Jovanovich.

Brown, Richard.

   100 Words About Animals. (1987). Harcourt Brace Jovanovich.

   100 Words About My House. (1988). Harcourt Brace Jovanovich.

   100 Words About Working. (1988). Harcourt Brace Jovanovich.

Ernst, Lisa Campbell. (1995). *Up to Ten and Down Again.* Mulberry.

Frith, Michael. (1973). *I'll Teach My Dog 100 Words.* Random House.

Hoban, Tana. (1987). *26 Letters and 99 Cats.* Greenwillow Press.

Kasza, Keiko. (1996). *The Wolf's Chicken Stew.* Putnam & Grosset.

LeSieg, Theodore. (1961). *Ten Apples Up on a Tree.* Random House.

Medearis, Angela Shelf. (1996). *The Hundredth Day of School.* Scholastic.

Merriam, Eve. (1993). *12 Ways to Get to 11.* Trumpet, Doubleday.

Pinczes. Eleanor. (1993). *One Hundred Hungry Ants.* Houghton Mifflin.

Ryan, Pan Munoz. (1994). *One Hundred is a Family.* Hyperion.

Spann, Mary. (1993). *Exploring the Numbers From 1-100.* Scholastic.

Viorst, Judith. (1980). *Alexander Who Used to be Rich Last Sunday.* Aladdin.

Williams, Rozanne. (1995). *The Bugs Go Marching In.* Creative Teaching Press.

Williams, Rozanne. (1995). *The Skip Count Book.* Creative Teaching Press.

Title: Memorable Summer Moment . . . What I Did on My Summer Vacation with a New Twist

Author: Tami J. Little

Big6 Skills: Big6 #3 Location & Access, Big6 #4–Use of Information, Big6 #5–Synthesis.

Learning Contexts: This project is applicable for language arts, social studies, and visual arts.

Discussion: In this lesson, students will collect, organize, prepare, and present materials in a scrapbook that represents their Memorable Summer Moment. At the beginning of each new school year, many students are required to write essays or stories titled, "My Summer Vacation." Too often, this exercise is a time filler that allows some children to brag and others to mourn. This lesson allows the students to extract relevant information and put it into a product that can be kept for years.

There is a scrapbooking craze in the craft world today. Often parents work hard to create the scrapbook, making sure it is perfect with journaling, artwork, and stickers to match. Children log their own memorable moments that may be very different from their parents.

The classroom teacher should send a letter to new students telling them about the assignment. This will allow students time to think about their memorable moment from summer. In the letter, the teacher should stress that this is not necessarily about a vacation or a trip. Examples of memorable moments are time in the park, playing at the pool, or swimming in the pond.

The teacher will send a letter (see the sample letter) to the students before the new school year begins. The students will determine some possible memorable summer moments with their parents and then gather photos, news clippings, postcards, or drawings to illustrate the moment. Students should bring in the materials during the first week of school.

The teacher discusses the Who, What, When, Where, and Why chart with the students. Students use the chart (see the sample) to brainstorm ideas about the memorable events. Students try to remember what was said, who said it, what they were thinking, feeling, wearing, or anything that made the moment memorable.

From this chart, the students are ready to create their scrapbook complete with journaling, pictures or graphics, and any other artwork they wish to include.

Example in Context:

The fourth grade teacher, the art teacher, and the librarian worked together on this project. The teacher wrote the letter to the students. She also taught the lesson on how to complete the Who, What, When, Where, and Why chart. The librarian showed the students examples of scrapbooking from her own personal pages as well as how to access a site for kids and scrapbooking on the Internet at URL: *http://www. jangle.com/* and *http://www.icanscrapbook.to/.* The librarian and the teacher worked together to help the students use their charts to make journal entries that connect the pictures and artwork to the memorable event.

The art teacher used this lesson to discuss shapes, lines, layout, and design. She showed the students how to make word art.

The students enjoyed the opportunity to scrapbook their memorable summer event. They learned about journaling and the importance of accuracy for anyone who might want to learn from it in the future. A scoring guide was the assessment used for this lesson. (See the sample.)

The teacher was able to use the lesson as a springboard for keeping a learning journal for recording important concepts learned throughout the school year. The librarian was able to use this lesson to tell students about books that have a journaling or diary format.

Memorable Summer Moment

Name: Mrs. Little

Directions: Complete the chart by answering each question. Be sure to include specific names, places, and dates. Try to remember exactly what was said, felt, or thought at the moment.

Who?	What?	When?	Where?	Why?
Joshua, Samantha, Ben, Krystal, Zalan, Grandma, and Mrs. Little	We went to the airport to say good-bye to Zalen.	Zalen left at 9:00 a.m., July 6, 1998.	Zalen left from the Sioux Gateway Airport near Sgt. Bluff, Iowa.	Zalen was an exchange student who lived in our home for a year. He had to return to Budapest, Hungary, to be with his family and friends. We all wanted to say good-bye to him because he was so special to us.

Notes: We were all feeling a little sad about Zalen having to leave. After all, he was part of our family. He walked outside and up the stairs of the airplane. He stepped into the plane. We were all sure that we would never see him again, when suddenly, he peeked his head out the door one more time, to wave another good-bye. Our whole family laughed in the airport at the silly boy who just had to see us one more time!

Memorable Summer Moment

Name:

Who?	What?	When?	Where?	Why?

Notes:

Names:

Who?	What?	When?	Where?	Why?

Notes:

Dear Parents,

Hello! I am your child's teacher for this school year. I am very excited to get to know you and your child. To break tradition from the "What I Did On My Summer Vacation" essay, I would like to take the time to do some creative scrapbooking with your child.

In case you have not heard of the term "scrapbooking," it simply means making a scrapbook. Scrapbooking can be anything from one event, one theme, or even one entire year. As a class, we are going to scrapbook "A Memorable Summer Moment." We will view some scrapbook pages on the Internet as well as some our librarian has created with her children. We will also do some journaling and create some artwork to illustrate the moments.

Your child needs to bring an idea to school! Talk with your child about this assignment. Have your child decide which moment was most memorable for the summer. Once the moment has been chosen, please help your child gather photos or news clippings, or encourage your child to make a drawing to illustrate the moment. Be sure that these are duplicate photos. Do not send priceless treasures, as these will not be returned in the original format.

Need some ideas for memorable moments? Here are just a few!
Summer carnival
A walk in the park
Fishing with Grandpa
Camping
The parade
The tornado
A trip to my cousins
Shopping for school clothes

If you have any questions, please don't hesitate to call or e-mail me. Thank you for your help with this assignment. Our memorable moments will be on display at the Back-to-School Night in October.

Sincerely,

Your Child's Teacher
<e-mail address>
<phone number>

Name: _____

Memorable Summer Moment
Self-Scoring Guide

Using the scoring guide below, evaluate your Memorable Summer Moment project. Below each of the statements, write *why* you gave yourself the score that you did.

5 = This is my best work.
4 = My work is good.
3 = My work is ok.
2 = My work needs improvement.
1 = I need to try again.

My Who, What, When, Where, and Why chart is complete.   5 4 3 2 1

I have included pictures, drawings, or graphics.   5 4 3 2 1

I have included word art that connects to my moment.   5 4 3 2 1

I have included journaling that I took from my chart.   5 4 3 2 1

Title: Presentation Pick: What's the Best Way to Present the Results of My Information Search?

Author: *Barbara A. Jansen*

Related Big6 Skills: *Big6 #5–Synthesis*

Purpose: *The purpose of this lesson is to introduce students to selecting the best presentation format.*

Learning Contexts: This lesson is applicable across subjects with students (grades 4–5) when introducing presentation format.

Discussion: This lesson will help students learn to choose the best product or performance for presenting information. Young learners (grades 4–5) need direct guidance when deciding which presentation format best presents the results of information searching. It is appropriate to assign a format, as teachers often use the presentation to teach production skills such as multimedia or word processing. Most young children in elementary school will create the presentation assigned by their teacher. However, as students enter fourth and fifth grades, they should have occasional opportunities to choose the format for presentation.

Sample in Context: Before participating in science lab activities, fifth grade students studying the properties of rocks and minerals were asked to provide their classmates with background information. Each group of students had one of these topics: igneous rocks, sedimentary rocks, metamorphic rocks, and minerals. Students helped generate the type of information they should locate (Big6

#1–Task Definition). Before continuing with the Big6 process, the teacher and library media specialist (LMS) discussed the final product so that students would have it in mind as they located information:

1. In group discussion, ask students what visuals or props they like when they see a live presentation. Make a list on the overhead or board. The teacher or LMS should add to the list any features that students do not identify, including visuals, audience participation, props, humor, and accurate content.

2. Ask students to brainstorm types of live presentations, again making a list. Examples may be skits, traditional transparencies with lecture, game show, newscast, puppet show, and many more. The teacher may want to add to the list.

3. Have each group of students match the presentations with the list of features and decide if the presentation allows for the inclusion of the features listed in #1.

4. Cross any presentations off the list that do not allow for an entertaining live presentation. Let each group choose a presentation format from the remaining list for the rock and mineral study that they will present to their classmates.

Title: Writing Physical Education Curriculum

Author: *Tami J. Little (original lesson idea by Rusty Peterson)*

Related Big6 Skills: *Big6 #4–Use of Information, and Big6 #5–Synthesis*

Purpose: *The students use lesson plans and ideas printed by the teacher and former students to create a three-week unit for sixth grade physical education.*

Learning Contexts: This lesson integrates technology, information, language and physical education.

Discussion: This lesson helps students learn how to gather and extract information from multiple sources. Many times, students feel they have little or no say in their own education either in content or delivery. This unit will allow students to develop curriculum. The students will create a lesson plan (see the sample) based on a given format. Groups of two or three students will write or word process the lessons for the three-week instructional unit.

The physical education teacher, librarian, and classroom teacher will work together to help students locate and access physical education lesson plans. Texts from education classes, teacher texts, and other books about games provide good resources for the students. Bookmark Internet sites to make access to the information simple and manageable. Encourage students to search using the Yahooligans search engine at *http://www.yahooligans.com*. Visit the following Internet Web sites:

http://ericir.syr.edu/Virtual/Lessons/Phys_Ed/index.html

http://discoveryschool.com/schrockguide/health/fitness.htm

http://pe.central.vt.edu

http://www.aahperd.org/

http://www.ping.be/sportsmedia/Lesson.htm

http://WWW.IDE.MAT-SU.K12.AK.US/pe/

http://www.stan-co.k12.ca.us/calpe

http://www.hillarysport.org.NZ

http://www.indiana.edu/~preschal/index.html

Sample in Context: Form groups of two to three students. Students will develop a three-week physical education curriculum unit for the sixth grade by using previously gathered material and material from Internet websites.

The criteria as listed in the scoring guide (see the sample) must be completed. Students will organize the gathered information on note cards, in an outline, or using a software program such as *Inspiration*.

Potential problems include: reaching group consensus on the activities, finding sufficient material that is appropriate for age and skill levels, and lacking equipment for some activities.

Each group will exchange its unit with another group and evaluate the proposed activities using the previously established criteria. The teacher will evaluate all proposals using the same criteria.

Follow-up activities will include the teacher randomly selecting and implementing a unit to see that all goes as planned. The teacher can have the students evaluate the unit after it was taught to see if it did work the way that they expected and to make any changes that would make it more successful in the future. Students could also look for information to teach younger children. The students could become PE buddies and help instruct the younger children. Students can also study developmentally appropriate activities by using the information found at the URL: *http://www.acs.ucalgary.ca/~jross/Developmental.html*

Physical Education Three-Week Unit Requirements

1. Activities must be conducted within the time constraints established by district policy: classes must be 25 minutes in length and will meet two to three days a week.

2. Only equipment presently on hand will be used for the activities.

3. Activities must be safe (as determined by the physical education teacher).

4. Each lesson plan must include activities for the development of endurance, strength, and coordination.

5. The plans must specify the type and amount of equipment needed, the area where the activity is to be conducted, and the size of the participant grouping (either in individual, twos, threes, teams, etc).

6. The teacher must determine if activities are appropriate for sixth grade students.

Physical Education Lesson Plan

Author:
Name of Activity:
Concept/Skill Being Taught:
Purpose of Activity:

- Endurance
- Strength
- Coordination

Prerequisites: (i.e., prior practice or learning needed, if any)

Time required:

Grouping:

- Individual
- Two
- Three
- Team
- Other

Where will the activity be played?:

Materials and equipment needed:

Description of activity:

Assessment ideas that evaluate if students reached the objectives:

Suggestions for adapting this activity for students with disabilities:

This lesson plan form is adapted with permission from PE Central at the URL:
http://pe.central.vt.edu/lessonideaform.html

REFLECTIONS

REFLECTIONS

CHAPTER 11

Big6™ Tips:
Evaluation – Ensuring
Effectiveness and Efficiency

The last stage of the Big6 is #6–**Evaluation.**

6.1 Judge the result (effectiveness).
6.2 Judge the process (efficiency).

Assessing effectiveness and efficiency of the process is crucial to success in information problem-solving. However, students often leave this step out—in part, because they are rarely taught to engage in self-assessment. Evaluation is a crucial component of the Big6 process. Students should be able to do the following:

- Engage in concrete tasks of reflecting and responding to predetermined criteria

- Determine the strengths and weaknesses of their solutions

- Justify their decisions based on criteria

- Understand the value of using a process to solve information problems, and

- Become self-directed and self-motivated to produce quality work.

Students need to learn to look at their work through their teachers' eyes.

When students evaluate themselves, they assume control and responsibility for their own work and become active participants in their learning. The role of the teacher becomes a guide, coach, and facilitator rather than the center of all knowledge and ultimate arbitrator.

Feelings are also important in evaluation. Students may lack confidence and pride in their work because they don't really know whether or not they have done a good job. Or, feelings of confidence and pride are replaced with frustration and disappointment when they get their assignment back with a poor grade when they expected to do well. From a Big6 perspective, we want students to apply the same evaluation criteria as teachers do to student work. Students need to learn to look at their work through their teachers' eyes. In this way, students can build on strengths and identify areas for improvement. Students gain insight into specific areas to improve their performance. This can boost confidence, pride, and result in a higher level of academic success.

Students of all ages can engage in evaluation activities. For example, with pre-K and kindergarten students, we teach "before you are about to turn in your work, stop a minute and think, 'Is this okay? Is this what I want it to be? Did I do what I was supposed to? Should I work a little more, make a change, do something else—or is it good enough?'"

The same review should be done with older students. Teach them to evaluate their process when they think they are ready to turn in a project. This reflection is a key part of students' improving as information problem solvers.

Effectiveness—6.1

Evaluating effectiveness means looking at the result, or culmination of the information problem-solving process. This result might be a paper, report, project, or even a test. Evaluating effectiveness means judging how well one did in meeting the goals of the information problem-solving process.

In effectiveness, students learn to judge their products. Students can learn to diagnose the result of their effort when they learn to do such things as the following:

- Compare the requirements to the results

- Check the appropriateness and accuracy of the information they use

- Judge how well their solution is organized

- Rate the quality of their final product or performance compared to their potential (i.e., Did I do the best that I could?), and

- Judge the quality of their product to a predefined standard.

Students can learn how to judge their own effectiveness. Some techniques to facilitate learning effectiveness include:

- Have students assess themselves before turning in their assignment. This will give them a basis to compare what they think versus what the teacher thinks.

- Use rubrics or scoring guides. Show students how you use these and then have students create scoring guides themselves.

- Have groups of students assess sample work that you provide—bad examples are often the best way to get students to recognize quality.

It is useful to help students think about effectiveness. This can be a tricky concept, but students of all ages can learn it. I like to start by using examples of effectiveness in other settings, such as sports and business. In sports, effectiveness means winning (and, of course, feeling okay about yourself). In business, effectiveness means making a profit (and also making a contribution to society). Discussing how to be effective in these situations gets students thinking about how they can be equally effective in school.

Efficiency—6.2

The other part of evaluating an information problem-solving process is thinking about efficiency. Efficiency means saving time and effort in the process. This is certainly something to which most students can relate.

Remind students that the goal in school is to do as well as possible with as little time and effort as possible. They may be surprised to hear that saving time and effort in schoolwork is okay as long as it results in a quality process. How can students be efficient and still be successful? The answer is, by honing their Big6 Skills.

Determining efficiency is as complex as dealing with effectiveness. Improving efficiency involves evaluating the nature, tendencies, and preferences of their personal information problem-solving process. This is sometimes referred to as "meta-cognition"—recognizing how we learn, process information, and solve problems. From a Big6 perspective, we can help students learn how to assess the efficiency of the process they use to reach decisions and solutions. Some techniques to facilitate learning and to evaluate

> *Remind students that the goal in school is to do as well as possible with as little time and effort as possible.*

efficiency include encouraging students to do the following:

- Keep a Big6 log of information problem-solving activities; periodically evaluate how you are doing

- Reflect back on the sequence of events and judge effort and time involved

- Review and analyze the areas of frustration and barriers they came up against, and

- Rate their abilities to perform specific information problem-solving activities (i.e., locating, note-taking, skimming, scanning, and prioritizing).

Here's a general TIP for improving both 6.1 and 6.2. For important assignments, I like to have students include a one-page assessment summary of their processes and the assignment. I want to know what worked and what didn't. If they could do it over, what would they do differently? If they could change one thing, what would it be? Then give credit for being insightful—after all, recognizing what one needs to do and to learn is most of the battle.

Title: Big6 Assessment Activity: Ask & Answer

Author: Mike Eisenberg

Related Big6 Skill: Big6 #6–Evaluation

Purpose: A technique that provides meaningful information to students about their own work.

Learning Contexts: "Ask & Answer" leads students to evaluate their own product and process. While the sample provided is aimed at middle-elementary-age students, it could be easily adjusted for various ages.

Discussion:

A practical, easy-to-implement technique that provides meaningful information to students about their own work is a simple "Ask & Answer" sheet (see sample Ask & Answer sheet). "Ask & Answer" helps students learn to evaluate their own product and process and reflect on how they might improve in the future. The key to "Ask & Answer" format is to pose meaningful questions that provide insight into both the content knowledge and information skills abilities. Some typical target questions that focus attention on specific aspects of the Big6 process include:

Task Definition:

■ Did I do what was asked?

■ Did I have enough information?

Information Seeking Strategies:

■ Were my information sources helpful?

■ Should I have found and used other sources?

Location & Access:

■ Was it easy to find sources and information within sources?

Use of Information:

■ Did I have trouble understanding the information in sources?

Synthesis:

■ How well is my project organized?

■ Did I have a good plan to organize my information or project?

■ Does my project include all the appropriate information I found?

Evaluation:

■ Is my project good; how do I know?

■ Am I proud of my project?

■ Am I proud of my effort?

■ What could I do better next time?

Raising self-assessment questions allows students to take time to reflect on what they have learned, their accomplishments, and areas for improvement. Students become comfortable with reflecting on their own abilities. Rather than passive reactors to teachers' assessments, they are active participants in judging their knowledge and skills.

Ask & Answer

How will I know I did a good job? (How will my teacher grade the assignment?)

1. _____

2. _____

3. _____

4. _____

5. _____

Did I do the best job I could?

How proud am I of my project?

How proud am I of my effort?

To get a better result next time, I could:

1. _____

2. _____

3. _____

4. _____

5. _____

Title: Bubbles, Evaluation: What Items Will Make Good Bubble Blowing Devices

Author: Tami J. Little

Related Big6 Skills: Big6 #2–Information Seeking Strategies, and Big6 #6–Evaluation

Purpose: This lesson will help students learn to predict, experiment, and then evaluate their prediction.

Learning Contexts: Students will discover that some predictions are correct, and some predictions are not correct. This lesson can provide a springboard for language arts, math, science, and social studies activities.

Discussion: The students will brainstorm ideas for what items will make good bubble blowing devices. The students will test their prediction by trying to blow bubbles with the items and then evaluate with (yes) if it worked, (no) if it did not.

The librarian will have a variety of items available at a table. Students and the librarian will look at each item and, as a class, predict if it will blow a bubble or not. Students will have a sheet in front of them to mark (yes) or (no), depending on what they believe will happen. Students will then go to the playground and try to blow bubbles with the items. Students will mark on their chart (yes) or (no) if the item worked or not. (See the sample chart.)

Sample in Context: Elementary school children need to be able to make predictions and then evaluate their predictions. Children are given the chart to complete. Using the chart, the students learn to predict, keep record of predictions, and evaluate their predictions.

The bubble lesson can extend to other scientific information such as colors and experiments on the consistency of the bubble mixture. Students could also create their own bubble blowing device by using pipe cleaners. This activity can transfer to math concepts such as the size and shapes of bubbles in relation to the size of the bubble blowing device.

Bubble Prediction

Directions: In the My Prediction column, write (yes) if you think the item will blow a bubble. Write (no) if you think the item will not blow a bubble. If the item does blow a bubble write (yes) in the Test column. If the item does not blow a bubble, write (no) in the Test column. How did you do? Did you predict correctly? In the evaluation column write (yes) if your prediction matched your test; write (no) if it did not.

Item	My Prediction	Test	Evaluation
Paper cup			
Hula hoop			
Straw			
Jar lid			
Fly swatter			
Wire whisk			
Scotch tape ring			
Pencil			
Marker lid			
Other			
Other			
Other			
Other			

Title: Self-Evaluation

Author: *Barbara A. Jansen*

Related Big6 Skills: *Big6 #6–Evaluation*

Purpose: *The purpose of this lesson is to help students think informally about their efforts in and the results of the information search process.*

Learning Contexts: This lesson is applicable across subject areas in elementary settings where students are finishing the Big6 process.

Discussion: In this lesson, students will learn to evaluate their own skills by responding to a set of questions for self-evaluation. Self-evaluation allows students to: determine whether or not they have completed the defined task, judge the efficiency of the entire process, and assess their personal information problem-solving styles. It allows students, teachers, and library media specialists to determine areas that need review and remediation. "Students' awareness of their strengths and weaknesses can lead, with instructional intervention, to overall improvements in their ability to solve future information problems," and promotes critical thinking (Eisenberg & Berkowitz 1990, p. 9).

Additionally, by posing some effective questions, students gain insight into interpersonal relationships and their ability to cooperate with others. Take, for example, this comment made by a gifted fifth grade girl who had recently enrolled in public school: "I found out a lot about group work. I found out that I can't always have my way. What I would do differently next time would be to think before I speak and to make suggestions instead of demands." A gifted boy, who worked cooperatively with a special education student said, "I found out that William is a pretty nice guy."

Sample in Context: Self-evaluation is the last step in the various information problem-solving process models. This step looks at the process and the results of the process—the product. It measures the effectiveness and efficiency of the information problem-solving process (Eisenberg & Berkowitz 1990, p. 9), taking place before the library media specialist and the teacher formally assess the assignment. In this phase, students look at the total picture. Which steps do the students feel competent and secure in and which are weak? Was the defined task accomplished? Students should think about what they learned that will apply to future learning so that they become aware of the transferability of the skills.

Giving students opportunities to write about their experiences encourages honest, critical evaluation of their own strengths and weaknesses. Providing students with written questions allows you to structure responses. The library media specialist and teacher should study the completed self-evaluation instruments, have conferences with students as needed, and make adjustments to future instruction.

Questions for final self-evaluation:

■ Is my assignment complete according to the defined task?

■ Did I give proper credit to my sources?

■ How efficient was I at choosing and finding my resources and which ones were useful?

■ Which resources did I need but could not find?

- What did I learn about the topic?

- Did I include in my final product or performance the things I found out about my topic?

- What did I learn how to do that I can use again?

- How can I use the skill again?

- How well did I do on my project? (The student can give himself/herself a rating or grade.)

- Did I write as little as possible when taking notes?

- Did I choose the best way to present my findings?

- Did I work well with my partners?

- Did I ask my teacher and library media specialist for help as needed?

- What materials were not available to me that I needed, or could have used?

- What could I do better next time?

Guidelines for Designing Student Self-Evaluation Instruments:

Keep the questions simple and developmentally appropriate. Keep in mind which content and processes you want the students to focus attention on and write questions accordingly. Ask questions to confirm the information problem-solving process as well as the final product so that students reflect on their personal styles. Be prepared to make adjustments in the lesson design and instructional delivery by using the results of student self-evaluation as a diagnostic tool.

Provide students with opportunities to evaluate their triumphs and obstacles as they progress through and complete the information problem-solving process. Then relax and watch as they become successful learners!

Name: _____

1. What did I learn?

2. What did I learn how to do that I can use again?

3. How can I use it?

4. How well did I do on my project?

| Great! I did my best work! | Pretty well. I almost did my best work. | Not very well. I could do better next time. | I did not try hard and did not do my best. |

5. Did I include the things I found out about my subject?

| Yes, I included everything | I left out a few things | I did not include everything |

6. Did I work well with my partner?

Yes!

Most of the time

No

7. What did I do well this time?

8. What could I do better next time?

9. What did I like most about doing this project?

Topic: _____

Big6™ Number Six—Evaluation

Name: _____

Project: _____

Now that you have finished your project, it is time to think about what you have accomplished. Please think about what you learned and the steps you followed in order to make your presentation. Write an evaluation of this experience, including the following:

- Your contribution to your group in finding information for the data chart and in preparing the presentation
- Your participation with your group
- What you learned (about the science content and in working with others)
- What you did well
- What you would do differently next time.

Please rate yourself on a scale of zero to ten (zero is low and ten is high)

- My contribution to the think cards _____
- My contribution to the presentation _____

Use the space below and on the back to write your self-evaluation.

REFLECTIONS

REFLECTIONS

TIPS for Introducing the "Super3" So...What About Working With the Very Youngest

This TIP focuses on what we consider to be the "Big6 Jr." —The Super3. The Super3 contains the same basic elements as the Big6, but makes the language and the concepts a little simpler and easier for younger students to understand. The Super3 are:

1. Plan – (Beginning)
2. Do – (Middle)
3. Review – (End).

This information problem-solving motto is easy to remember, fun to say, and helps young students get a handle on information problem-solving.

The importance of the Super3 lies in the fact that it gets the youngest students to start thinking in terms of process. Many students are not able to see past the Do component of the process when thinking about the work that they do in school or any other information problem-solving activity. While Do is an important step in creating a product or solving

> *To get your young students thinking in terms of process, have them imagine themselves as the main character in a story about completing the task at hand.*

a problem, it cannot exist on its own. Do works the best when it falls between plan and review.

To get your young students thinking in terms of process, have them imagine themselves as the main character in a story about completing the task at hand. This is a concept that every student will be able to grasp, since students hear stories all of the time. Now have them explain the plot line of the story; how do they prepare to tackle the assignment, problem, or task? After they describe finishing the task, have them consider whether or not this was a good story. Did the central character do a good job? Once students become comfortable with identifying the elements of the Super3, make a habit of regularly asking students to identify the Super3 steps in every story that you read together as a class. You will be surprised by how quickly they will "get" it!

Plan (Beginning) is the important first step of the Super3, and it is a step that students don't always take naturally. More often, they jump right into the middle and begin doing their assignments. The key is getting them to think about their planning process and to understand its importance. When kindergartners are given a picture to color, spend a moment with them discussing the step that they take in choosing colors. What are they doing when they choose the blue crayon for the sky? They are planning how they will tackle the assignment to achieve the desired effect. This is really no different from a twelfth grader planning which resources she will consult first when writing her term paper about Hamlet. Helping your students begin to think in terms of process creates the foundation for educational success throughout their school career.

Young elementary students do a great deal of planning in their daily routine. This includes:

- Choosing teams for a kickball game
- Picking blocks to use to build a castle
- Selecting a picture book to check out from the library media center
- Deciding where to place their mat for naptime.

Planning is a natural function of human thought. It is your responsibility as an educator to help students see the importance of the planning process.

Review (End) is a more difficult concept for most students to remember. Many kids feel that once they complete a task or assignment, their job is done. However, to truly build a foundation for academic success, young students must not forget to evaluate what they have produced. Just as Big6 #6–Evaluation—asks students to evaluate both process and product, Review is a multi-faceted concept as well. When asking students about their work, don't just ask them if

Ask them about the path that they took to complete the assignment and whether or not they would do it differently next time.

they created a quality product. Ask them about the path that they took to complete the assignment and whether or not they would do it differently next time.

One way to get your students into the Review habit is to make it a part of your assignments. When planning an activity, build in evaluation time. Have students look over their work before they turn it in, and put their initials on the back of the paper if they believe that what they created meets the assignment. Be very specific and clear about your expectations when assigning work to your students since this will give them a better foundation for reviewing the work that they have done.

Encourage parents to make evaluation a part of students' home life, too. Talk to parents about the importance of Review at parents' night. Occasionally send students home with a piece of paper for their parents, explaining what the students learned and did in class that day. Have parents ask their children specific questions about what they learned in class and whether or not they feel they did a good job on their assignment. This will avoid the "'What did you learn at school today?' 'Nothing'" syndrome at the dinner table and will help reinforce the importance of Review outside of the classroom.

To see the Super3 in action, let's take an example of an assignment given to a kindergarten class. Students are to work with a partner to draw a picture showing five winter activities. Let's see how the Super3 could be applied. Are partners talking about which winter activities to include? (Plan). What about actually working on the project? (Do). How about looking over their picture before they turn it in? (Review). The Super3 is super easy and will put your little ones on the road to success!

Working with Young Children: Hints from Other Educators

Many elementary educators have sent us helpful hints for ways they've worked with their young audiences on the Big6 and Super3. The following messages received via e-mail and the Big6 listserv, represent a few of the exciting ideas we've received.

Dale Lyles, of Newnan, Georgia, uses the Big6 for all elementary students instead of starting with the Super3 and working up to the Big6. Dale suggests translating the Big6 into simpler statements and questions that even the youngest students would be able to understand. For instance, instead of: Task Definition: Define the problem and Identify the information needed, Dale uses 1. Task Definition: What do I need to do?

Also, rather than insisting that her students memorize the Big6, Dale makes sure that the Big6 is posted so that students can see it and refer to it easily. Students will know the Big6 like the back of their hands before long!

Barbara Jansen also offers some great advice for using the Big6 with younger students. She sent a message to the Big6 listserv explaining that when she teaches the Big6 to teachers, she urges them to stress three things with their students. The first is awareness—it is important to point out to students when they use Big6 Skills. For instance, a student is not just typing a paper in the computer lab—they are Synthesizing (Big6 #5)! The second is developmental appropriateness—make sure that you are teaching the Big6 to students in a way that they can grasp. Finally, Barbara urges teachers to have fun with the Big6 so they can communicate to students that the information problem-solving process is an enjoyable one. Awareness—appropriateness—fun. Good advice to guarantee successful Big6/Super3 learning.

> *Dale Lyles, of Newnan, Georgia, uses the Big6 for all elementary students instead of starting with the Super3 and working up to the Big6.*

Mary Croix Ludwick, a library media specialist from The Colony, Texas, has a Location & Access unit for teaching third graders about the Dewey Decimal System, card catalogs, and electronic catalogs that follows Barbara's guidelines. This unit could be taught as part of a major research project or literature project.

Mary begins the first unit by making her students be books. She gives her students poster-board "spines" with call numbers on them. Three students begin the activity by coming to the front of the room and arranging themselves on the "shelf." The rest of the class joins them in groups of three until the entire class is arranged on the shelf. The students then take these "books" to the library shelves to find where the book would have actually gone, had they had been a real book.

Next, Mary teaches her students about card catalogs and electronic catalogs. Using photocopied catalog cards of actual books in the school library, Mary teaches her students to understand the information on the card. The students then use the cards to find the books and compare the information on the card with that in the book. They then apply these same skills to the electronic card catalog. Is the information housed within the catalog a good description of the book? How can we use the catalog to find a book?

After Mary's students have learned all about classification, catalogs, and shelf placement, she has them actually shelve books. When they are able to shelve to her satisfaction, Mary pronounces them knowledgeable about shelf placement (imagine the wonderful crowns or other prizes that you could make for the students when you pronounce them Masters of the Dewey Decimal System!). From this point on, whenever Mary's students return a book to the library, they re-shelve it themselves.

Lynn Spencer, Syracuse, New York, says, "To be honest, I keep working away at this trying to get it (Big6) right for the grade levels that I work with. I have a wonderful supporter in this quest—a first grade teacher who has a room right next to the library. This past year, Becky and I tried using the K-W-L model, but we weren't satisfied with that either. We really don't think that very young children need to think so much about "What I Know" because they usually think this is a lot more than what they actually do know. And it also gets in the way of their really searching for the needed information. This year the first grade teacher and I gave them a writing/drawing "journal" for their animal research, and I am providing them with a wide range of materials (CD-ROMs, Internet sites, etc.) for the research phase (they are working with parent helpers). The final product is a KidPix slide show created by the whole class.

Title: Curious George and the Super3

Author: Ann Gray, Pittsburg School, Pittsburg, New Hampshire

Related Big6 Skills: Super3

Purpose: The purpose of this lesson is to use a familiar children's story to introduce students to the Super3 concept.

Learning Contexts: This lesson is applicable with students in early elementary grades (pre-K–1) when introducing Super3 concepts.

Discussion: I had discussed the Super3 with the first graders a few weeks ago so they knew all of the steps, but we hadn't talked about it in a while. Then, the other day I was reading H.A. Rey's book, *Curious George Gets a Medal*, when I spotted a perfect opportunity to share how the Super3 worked for George. If you're familiar with the story, you know George gets into his usual series of scrapes. In fact, he has a lot of problems that he tries to solve. In each case, he "plans" out a solution to his problem, he "does" (or follows through with) his solution, and then he is forced to "review" when the solution doesn't actually solve the problem. I think just about any of the Curious George stories could work to emphasize the Super3 with the younger students.

REFLECTIONS

CHAPTER 13

Closing

The Pervasive Big6

Our work with the Big6 has resulted in our seeing the world through "Big6 glasses." In other words, it seems that we are constantly coming across events and actions that relate to the Big6 in every area of life. This shouldn't come as a great surprise, because there is growing recognition of the extent to which information literacy and information skills pervade everyday life.

This fact was made clear in an episode of the television cartoon show *The Simpsons*. In this episode, Bart must learn to play miniature golf to prepare for a competition. He is at a complete loss about how to approach the problem and turns to his sister, Lisa, for help. A trip to the library gives them the information they need to make Bart a successful miniature golfer. In solving this information problem, the Simpson children use all stages of the Big6:

- **Task Definition—focusing on the problem and the information requirements**
- **Information Seeking Strategies—using the library**

Remember, Bill Gates recently stated that computing power has increased 1 million times over the past 20 years and will likely do so again in the next 20 years!

- **Location & Access—using the library catalog**
- **Use of Information—reading and sharing the information**
- **Synthesis—applying "geometry" to the golf problem**
- **Evaluation—realizing that it worked.**

Another example of the widespread applicability of the Big6 is in the movie *Apollo 13*. In one part of the film, a broken air filter threatens to cause the spacecraft to run out of breathable air. To save the astronauts' lives, the ground crew must make a different type of air filter work in place of the broken one by using only the materials the astronauts have available. After a good deal of experimentation, the ground crew solves the information problem just in time. As with the *Simpsons* example, the people in the *Apollo 13* film can be seen using all of the Big6 steps with special emphasis on Task Definition, Information Seeking Strategies, Use of Information, and Synthesis. Solving this information problem is one of the most exciting points in the movie.

Use of the Big6 can also be seen in sporting events. A football game, for instance, is essentially an information problem—pitting one information system against another. In order to win, the coaches need to gather, assess, and synthesize information from the situation (such as weak areas of the other team and strengths of his/her own team) and use this information to devise a winning strategy (for example, which play to run). Ultimate evaluation is very easy to determine—check the scoreboard at the end of the game.

The idea that "information is everywhere" is the basis of our view of information literacy. Information is a pervasive and essential part of our society, and indeed, our lives. We are, at our essence, processors and users of information. This is not a recent development. Humans have always been dependent upon information to help make decisions and guide our actions. Change has come in the sheer volume of information and the complexity of information systems—largely due to advances in information technology and the accelerated rate at which we live our lives. Remember, Bill Gates recently stated that computing power has increased 1 million times over the past 20 years and will likely do so again in the next 20 years!

Recognizing the pervasive nature of information and the importance of information problem-solving skills is the key to where we, as educators, are and where we are going. It is our responsibility to understand the nature of information and the way that people use it. We can ensure that all individuals have the opportunity to learn the information literacy skills they will need in the future to successfully navigate the future landscape of information.

Summary

Information problem-solving is a basic component in effective instructional programs.
The Big6 Approach to Information Problem-Solving:

■ Level 1: Information Problem-Solving
Whenever students are faced with an information problem (or with making a decision that is based on information), they can use a systematic, problem-solving process.

■ Level 2: The Big6 Skills
1. Task Definition
2. Information Seeking Strategies
3. Location & Access
4. Use of Information
5. Synthesis
6. Evaluation

■ Level 3: Components of the Big6 Skills
1. Task Definition:
   1.1 Define the problem
   1.2 Identify the information requirements of the problem
2. Information Seeking Strategies:
   2.1 Determine the range of possible sources
   2.2 Evaluate the different possible sources to determine priorities
3. Location & Access:
   3.1 Locate sources
   3.2 Find information within sources
4. Use of Information:
   4.1 Engage (e.g., read, hear, view) the information in a source
   4.2 Extract information from a source
5. Synthesis:
   5.1 Organize information from multiple sources
   5.2 Present information
6. Evaluation
   6.1 Judge the product
   6.2 Judge the information problem-solving process.

The benefits of the Big6 Skills' broad-based approach to information problem-solving include the following:

■ Improved instructional practices

■ Provision for individualization and adaptability of the process to all students' learning styles

■ Clear definition of the requirements of good units and lessons from an information perspective

■ Provision of a framework for the analysis of existing instructional units and lessons

■ Provision of a structure for results-based assessments.

REFLECTIONS

REFLECTIONS

Comparison of Information Skills Process Models (Adapted from Eisenberg & Brown [1992])

Kuhlthau Information Seeking Process	Eisenberg/Berkowitz Information Problem-Solving	Irving Information Skills (The Big6 Skills)	Pitts/Stripling Research Process	New South Wales Information
1. Initiation 2. Selection	1. Task Definition 1.1 Define the problem 1.2 Identify info requirements	1. Formulation/analysis of information need	1. Choose a broad topic 2. Get an overview of the topic 3. Narrow the topic 4. Develop thesis/ purpose statement	Defining
1. Formulation (of focus)				
3. Exploration (investig. info on the general topic) 5. Collection (gather info on the focused topic)	2. Information Seeking Strategies 2.1 Determine range sources 2.2 Prioritize sources	2. Identification/appraisal of likely sources	5. Formulate questions to guide research 6. Plan for research & production	Locating
	3. Location & Access 3.1 Locate sources 3.2 Find info	3. Tracing/locating indiv. resources 4. Examining, selecting, & rejecting indiv. resources	7. Find, analyze, evaluate resources	Selecting
	4. Information Use 4.1 Engage (read, view, etc.) 4.2 Extract info	5. Interrogating/using individ-ual resources 6. Recording/storing info	8. Evaluate evidence take notes/compile bib.	Organizing
6. Presentation	5. Information Use 5.1 Organize 5.2 Present	7. Interpretation, analysis, synthesis and eval. of info. 8. Shape, presentation, and communication of info	9. Formulate questions to guide research 10. Create and present final product	Presenting
7. Assessment (of outcome/process)	6. Evaluation 6.1 Judge the product 6.2 Judge the process	9. Evaluation of the assignment	(Reflection point—is the paper/project satisfactory)	Assessing

Spitzer, K. L., Eisenberg, M. B. & Lowe, C. A. (1998). Information Literacy: Essential Skills for the Information Age. (pp.68-69). Syracuse, NY: ERIC Clearinghouse on Information and Technology. Reprinted with permission.

Big6™ Song

Big6 Song

(Sung to the tune of "B-I-N-G-O")
words by Barbara A. Jansen

There is a process I can use and Big6 is its name-O

Refrain:
B-I-G S-I-X, B-I-G S-I-X, B-I-G S-I-X
And Big6 is its name-O.

Big6 One will help me find out just what I should do-O (refrain)
Big6 Two will help me choose those things that I should use-O (refrain)
Big6 Three will help me get those things that I will need-O (refrain)
Big6 Four helps me to take out words that I can use-O (refrain)
Big6 Five helps me finish the work that I must do-O (refrain)
Big6 Six helps me to know if I did my best work-O (refrain)

References

American Association of School Librarians and Association of Educational Communications and Technology. (1998). *Information power: Building partnerships for learning.* Chicago: American Library Association.

Ball, L. (1952). [video]. *I Love Lucy: The classics: V.6.* (ASIN: 6304872607). (Available from Amazon.com, http://www.amazon.com)

Barry, C. L. (1994, Apr). User-Defined relevance criteria: An exploratory study. *Journal of the American Society for Information Science, 45* (3), 149-59.

Drucker, P. (1992, December 1). Be data literate—know what to know. *Wall Street Journal,* p. A16.

Eisenberg, M. B., & Berkowitz, R. E. (1996). *Helping with homework: A parent's guide to information problem-solving.* Syracuse, NY: ERIC Clearinghouse on Information & Technology.

Eisenberg, M. B., & Berkowitz, R. E. (1990). *Information problem-solving: The Big Six skills approach to library and information skills instruction.* Norwood, NJ: Ablex.

Gross, M. (1998). Imposed Queries in the School Library Media Center: A Descriptive Study. *Dissertation Abstracts International, 59*(09), 3261. (University Microfilms No. 9905536).

Information Fatigue Syndrome. (1996, October 1). *Investor's Business Daily.*

Jansen, B. (1997, Nov/Dec). "TIPS#1: Teaching Information Problem-Solving: The Trash-N-Treasure note-taking technique," *The Big6 Newsletter, 1*(2), 13.

Jansen, B. A. (1996, Feb). Reading for information: The Trash-'n-Treasure method of teaching notetaking. *School Library Media Activities Monthly, 12*(6), 29-32.

Koberg, D., & Bagnall, J. (1980). *The universal traveler, A Soft-systems guide to creativity, problem-solving and the process of reaching goals.* William Kaufmann, Inc.

Kuhlthau, C. C. (1993). Implementing a process approach to information skills: A study identifying indicators of success in library media programs. *School Library Media Quarterly, 22*(1), 11-18.

Kuhlthau, C. C. (1985). *Teaching the library research process.* West Nyack, NY: The Center for Applied Research in Education.

Large, P. (1984). *The micro revolution, revisited.* Rowman & Littlefield. (ISBN: 0847673618).

Naisbitt, J. (1982). *Megatrends: Ten new directions transforming our lives.* New York, NY: Warner Books.

Noller, Parnes, and Biondi. (1976). Creative problem solving model. In *Creative behavior workbook.* New York: Scribner.

Pappas, M., & Tepe, A. (1997*). Pathways to knowledge: Follet's information skills model kit.* McHenry, IL: Follett Software.

Rappa, M., (Ed.). (1998). *CyberScape Digest.* Faulkner Information Services. [Online]. Available: http://www.cs.cmu.edu/afs/cs.cmu.edu/user/bam/www/numbers.html#Internet. [1998, April 17].

Stripling, B. K. & Pitts, J.M. (1988). *Brainstorms and blueprints: Teaching library research as a thinking process.* Englewood, CO: Libraries Unlimited.

Wurman, R. S. (1989). *Information anxiety.* New York: Doubleday.

Subject Index Compiled by Kathleen L. Spitzer